"This is a brutally honest sonal struggle with the w that life-changing experie._ _ bat-weary veteran as well as his persistently supportive spouse, this is one of the only books I've ever read that succinctly addresses the impact of post-traumatic stress on veterans as well as their family members. I highly recommend this book for both the academic environment and as a personal read for veterans attempting to find their way back home to a new orientation from the battlefield. Anyone with a heart of compassion for the incalculable sacrifices made by the members of the United States Armed Services will find this book extremely helpful in providing pastoral care and personal support to our wounded warriors."

Douglas L. Carver, Chaplain (Major General),
U.S. Army, Retired
Former U.S. Army Chief of Chaplains

"Mike and Kathy Langston share their journey of post traumatic stress recovery uniquely from perspectives of a healer/wounded warrior and his family; highlighting the need to address the intertwined wounds of both spirit and mind to restore health. Those struggling with PTSD, their loved ones, and their caregivers will benefit from this brave and insightful book. Both Mike and Kathy are excellent writers. I love the way that they have woven together input from themselves and the family. I found the reference to Mike's experience on the cliffs in Iceland where the wind lifted him to be especially powerful."

Heidi A. Fowler, M.D.
Psychiatrist
Captain, Medical Corps, U.S. Navy, Retired

"This is a personal and deeply moving account of the effects of PTSD on marriage, family and faith. Candid and haunting, the book recounts the experience of those who return home fighting the war within. For those, like me, engaged in full-time ministry, it is essential reading."

Derek W. H. Thomas, Ph.D.
Senior Minister, First Presbyterian Church, Columbia, SC
Robert Strong Professor of Systematic and Pastoral Theology,
Reformed Theological Seminary, Atlanta, and
Teaching Fellow, Ligonier Ministries

"Drs. Michael W. and Kathy J. Langston offer a courageous and transparent account of how persons and their families experiencing post-traumatic stress disorder experience orientation, disorientation, and reorientation with accompanying intensity, severity, and duration that rocks one's identity and every relationship including that with the divine. With stereophonic voicing this couple presents their journey together to find how to make meaning when traditional care omits or minimizes the spiritual aspects needed to journey through the dark night of the soul.

Emphasizing the primacy of the returning servicemen and women's sharing their personal narrative as part of the healing process, this book demonstrates how there are no easy answers or pious platitudes. Instead, common road markers along the journey exist to assist in becoming an authentic seeker. This story is set in the context of a military family and shows how PTSD affects spouses and children as well as service personnel. The Langstons offer a wonderful gift to all warriors and those laity and professionals who seek to stand with them and offer care."

James W. Pruett, D.Min., Ph.D., LPC, LMFT, LPCS, LMFTS, CFBPPC
President, Academy for Wellness, Education
and Services Training Program
Founder, Integrative Psychotherapy Training Program,
Carolinas Healthcare System Chair, Membership Division,
American Association of Pastoral Counselors

"*A Journey to Hope* is a very thorough case study of a military chaplain who develops PTSD (as a result of multiple deployments to the Middle East, including one in which he spent twenty-four months of the thirty-month assignment in a combat zone) and the effects that it had on him and his family. As the war on terror continues and our military's deployments to hazardous areas of the world continue, our society needs to be better informed on what PTSD does to our wounded warriors and their families. This is the story of how one senior military chaplain and his family have coped utilizing clinical and theological/faith resources. This is not a light read. But it is a very important one, and it should be considered mandatory reading for all military chaplains as well as for psychotherapists and others who work with military personnel, veterans, and their families."

The Reverend David Plummer
Former U.S. Army chaplain
Licensed Psychotherapist/Psychotherapy Supervisor
Ecclesiastical Endorser, The Coalition of Spirit-filled Churches

"American warriors are not immune to compassion fatigue, burnout, moral injury, vicarious traumatization, and post-traumatic stress as they serve in a unique environment that includes frequent exposure to trauma. Whether the trauma was experienced directly or indirectly during wartime or peace, hidden wounds and injuries often result. Mike and Kathy Langston have given all warriors and their family members a valuable gift through sharing their transparent journey to hope and healing in this must-read book. This book strengthened our marriage by giving us faith, hope, and encouragement that we could experience peace and healing from the pain that war and trauma places on warriors and their family members. We highly recommend this book to every military service member and their spouse!"

Chaplain, Lt Col Brian Bohlman, ANG
Author, *For God and Country:
Considering the Call to Military Chaplaincy*

Shelley Bohlman, military spouse of over 20 years
Co-Founder of Operation ThankYou.org

"In this candid and revealing account, readers are given a glimpse into the impact of the unseen wounds of war on an individual, a spouse, children, and the relationships of marriage and family. Guidance is provided to assist in the journey that is necessary to see spiritual healing begin for those wounded and to cope with the continued intrusion of these wounds into the lives of the individuals affected.

Through the Langston's stories we come to understand that traumatized warriors and their loved ones can lose perspective of their hope and question their faith. But we also learn from their insights and counsel that there is a Comforter who has been sent to lead us to a deepening and vital relationship with God, our Father, who loves us with an all-encompassing, long-suffering, never-ending love, and who provides us hope in Jesus Christ, the Author and Perfecter of our faith."

The Reverend James E. Watson, Ph.D.
Professor, Columbia International University
Columbia, South Carolina

A JOURNEY TO
HOPE

Healing the Traumatized Spirit

Michael W. Langston, DMin
CAPT, CHC, USN (Ret.)

Kathy J. Langston, PhD

A JOURNEY TO HOPE: Healing the Traumatized Spirit
Copyright © 2016 Michael W. Langston and Kathy J. Langston
All rights reserved.

No part of this book may be reproduced in any form or by any electronic or mechanical means including information storage and retrieval systems, without permission in writing from the author. The only exception is by a reviewer, who may quote short excerpts in a review.

Lampion Press, LLC
P. O. Box 932
Silverton, OR 97381

ISBN: 978-1-942614-14-2

Library of Congress Control Number: 2015960623

Formatting and cover design by Amy Cole, JPL Design Solutions

Printed in the United States of America

This book is dedicated to:

Rear Admiral Robert F. Burt, CHC, USN
24th Chief of Navy Chaplains
(1948 – 2014)

Whose inspirational leadership and courage
provided our Navy's Chaplain Corps
with guidance and mentorship
during America's wars
in Afghanistan and Iraq.
His life as a man of faith
who continually relied on his Lord
serves as an example to all chaplains.

This book also stands as a remembrance of
the 112 Marines, sailors, and soldiers
who gave their lives for our country
in Al Anbar Province, Iraq,
January 2007 through
February 2008.

Table of Contents

Introduction 1

**Chapter One: "Eternal Father, Strong to Save,
Whose Arm Dost Bind the Restless Wave"** 5
    Post Traumatic Stress Disorder (PTSD) 7
    Trauma 9
    Posttraumatic Growth (PTG) and Spiritual Health 11
    The Navy Hymn as a Framework 15
    An Added Note 17

Chapter Two: "Protect the Ones We Love at Home" 19
    U.S. Marine Corps Infantry Officer 20
    U.S. Navy Chaplain 22
        MCAS New River, NC 23
        Desert Shield/Desert Storm 24
        USS *Chosin (CG 65) Pearl Harbor, Hawaii* 28
        NWS Yorktown, VA 29
        NAS Keflavik, Iceland 30
        Camp Lejeune, NC 31
        NS Newport, RI 31
        NS Norfolk, VA 32
        CFC-A Kabul, Afghanistan 32
        Camp Fallujah, Iraq 35

Chapter Three: "O Hear Us When We Cry to Thee" 41
    Times of Stress and Danger 42

Times of Confusion and Dismay 44
II Marine Expeditionary Force Forward Chaplain 46
PTSD Never Just Simmers 48
Commanding Officer: Naval Chaplaincy
   School and Center 50
Respite from the War: A Beginning 55

Chapter Four: "For Those in Peril on the Sea" 57
Counseling: First Round 58
Graduation Day 67
   Kathy 68
   Mike 69

Chapter Five: "Our Brethren Shield in Danger's Hour" 71
Combat Stress and Trauma 74
Proximity, Intensity, and Duration 79
Trauma's Effects on the Body and Mind 82
Trauma's Effects on the Spirit 92

Chapter Six: "Most Holy Spirit Who Didst Brood Upon the Chaos Dark and Rude" 97
Intensity, Severity, and Duration 97
Historical Approaches 99
Danger's Effects on the Mind and Body 100
Existential Existence 102
PTSD Descriptions 104
Beginnings 106
Table 1: Combat Skills and Responses in
   Combat Zone and at Home 112

Chapter Seven: "And Bid Its Angry Tumult Cease" 117
Adjusting to Home 119
Changing Bit by Bit 124
Lesson 1: Safe at Home 129
   Step 1: Word Choice 130
   Step 2: Slowing Down 131
   Step 3: Safe Spaces 132

    Lesson 2: Order and Structure 133
    Lesson 3: Accommodations 134
        Step 1: Immediate Family 134
        Step 2: Extended Family 135
        Step 3: Lessen Stress 135
    Respite 135

Chapter Eight: "And Hushed Their Raging at Thy Word" 141
    Counseling 143
    Chaos and Confusion 145
    Therapy and Narratives 148
        Reconstructing the Trauma Story 149
        Establishing Safety 150
        Restoring Connections 152

Chapter Nine: "Protect Them Wheresoe'er They Go" 155
    "I Have Severe PTSD" 159
    Spiritual Wound 161
        Authentic Seeker 163
        Opening to the Spirit 166
        Dark Night of the Soul 169
    Resilience and Posttraumatic Growth (PTG) 173

Chapter Ten: "And Give, for Wild Confusion, Peace" 181
        Kathy 181
        Mike 182

Appendix A **189**

Appendix B **191**

Appendix C **197**

Appendix D **201**

References **203**

Biographies **207**

Introduction

~

We are a family living with the after-effects of the wars in Afghanistan and Iraq. After spending twenty-four of thirty months in the combat zone, Mike returned home with a diagnosis of Post Traumatic Stress Disorder (PTSD). Even though Mike had been deployed (sent on assignments) for nine of our twenty-five years of married life in the military, we were ill equipped for his return from the combat zone. We share our story in this book in order that others who live with the after-effects of these wars may be able to find their way to healing and hope.

As a Christian family, we offer a journey to healing that relies on guidance from the Holy Spirit. We know no other way to share our lives and our struggles except through the relationship we have with God through His Son, Jesus Christ. We offer an arduous journey that requires warriors to move bit-by-bit out of the protective shells that kept them alive in the combat zone. In order to accomplish this task, warriors need the help of a trusted friend or family member. Thus, our story is for both warriors and those who love them.

If, like us, you have tried to find your way back to "what was before the war" or tried to establish a "new normal" with few differences, then we encourage you to journey with us as we explore Charles Hoge's explanations of how warriors react in the combat zone. In *Once a Warrior Always a Warrior,* Hoge explains how this "locked and loaded" survival behavior in the combat zone produces more than a few awkward situations at home. We offer an interpretative table contrasting the combat skill and combat behavior with the action at home and the warriors' thoughts. This table is the beginning of understanding what warriors are experiencing as they return home. Those warriors who find their dreams and thoughts remain in the combat zone can (though not always) receive a PTSD diagnosis. This table is a beginning point for those who love warriors to understand their behaviors and motivations.

Understanding can bring change. Change can bring hope. Hope can bring healing. The chaos in the minds of warriors and the painful memories they bring home can overwhelm the warrior's abilities to cope in the more mundane world of "home." We offer our story of how we learned to understand the after-effects of war and the changes in our home that provided Mike with a safe environment with the hope that other families struggling with these after-effects can find their way to a healing journey as well.

We base our story in our Christian faith; yet, we do not confine this story to just Christians. Providing a safe place for warriors to live is a key element in relaxing survival instincts when warriors return home. Many books on the market at this time offer the advice of spouses or warriors putting on the armor of God (Ephesians 6) in order to fight this spiritual battle of PTSD. Warriors already have on armor, but this armor is for self-protection—a needed skill in the combat zone. Spouses, suited up ready for battle, will find a war with the warrior, but it will not be a productive spiritual war. Both of these battles are counterproductive to spiritual healing.

The spiritual journey to which God calls us is one that demands surrendering our armor in order to stand defenseless before Him. In this way, we learn dependence on Him. God is in control and He brings healing to the spiritual wounds that war inflicts. We, as people dealing with the effects of PTSD, must learn to surrender to His leadership and guidance. We use Walter

Brueggemann's concepts of "orientation—disorientation—reorientation" (2002, p. x) to explain the process of leaving the world of orientation, moving to a state of disorientation within the combat zone, and finding hope through a new orientation that the Holy Spirit provides for us.

Our story is a positive one. Our story is one of hope and healing. We share this story with the hope that those who have been diagnosed with PTSD, those who know someone with PTSD, or those who live with someone with PTSD can find a way to ease their pain and calm the storm within their homes. There is hope. Healing is possible. As we share our journey, it is our sincere prayer that our journey will help you on yours.

CHAPTER ONE

"Eternal Father, Strong to Save, Whose Arm Dost Bind the Restless Wave"

∽

This is a story of hurting, healing, and hope. This story is our declaration that our eternal Father IS strong to save and that He continually binds the restless waves that pound the minds, hearts, and spirits of our warriors returning from Afghanistan, Iraq, and other areas of conflict throughout the world. He also binds the waves for any traumatized person who turns to Him. We are Christians and relate this journey through our Christian perspective, but the truths of this journey are timeless. Through our family's story, we present how Post Traumatic Stress Disorder (PTSD) disrupts the households of warriors throughout our nation. As we explain PTSD and the disruptions that occur, we weave our family's story into the information.

Our primary purpose is to share the journey to physical, mental, and spiritual healing on which our family embarked. That long journey led us to hope and peace. We share this story now with the prayer that those traumatized by war and other horrors can begin their own journeys to healing their traumatic wounds. We share our story so that families can understand the motivations of warriors and through that understanding provide a needed safe place for warriors to heal. No easy answers or quick fixes are within this book. We do not present a path back to an old life that existed before deployments. We also do not seek a "new normal." We offer an approach that echoes the journeys of so many throughout the decades. This journey brings warriors, traumatized individuals, and families face-to-face with their wounds which results in encountering our eternal Father. The journey is one that requires faith and trust. The rewards are immeasurable.

We are a family who has, for more than a decade, dealt directly with the effects of the wars in Afghanistan and Iraq either through deployments or through the after effects of those deployments. My husband, Mike, retired as a Navy Captain in 2011 after thirty years of active service in both the Navy and the Marine Corps. From August 2005 until May 2008, Mike spent twenty-four of thirty months in the combat zone. His ministry included first working as Theater Chaplain for Combined Forces Command–Afghanistan (CFC–A). During that year he also worked with and mentored the Afghan Minister of Hajj and Islamic Affairs in Kabul, Afghanistan. Upon coming home from Afghanistan, Mike was assigned to be the Force Chaplain for II Marine Expeditionary Forces, Al Anbar Province, Iraq.

When Mike came home, he had difficulty slowing down from the up-tempo pace that had kept him alive in the combat zones. He retired three years after returning to the U.S. and was, at the time of his retirement, diagnosed with severe Post Traumatic Stress Disorder (PTSD). This book is about our experiences living with and moving through PTSD to posttraumatic growth (PTG) with an added spiritual element. Through understanding how the war affected Mike and then our family, we have learned many skills to help us find a path to hope and healing, primarily through spiritual resources. This book is our journey through Mike's wartime wound and into the spiritual growth and understanding that comes with posttraumatic growth and spiritual health.

We bring our story to the overflow of PTSD books and articles because we have a more unique perspective than many people who write. Many of the books, articles, and studies are by those on the "outside looking in." These are the psychiatrists, psychologists, social workers, therapists, and others who are non-military and have gained knowledge only by observing and not by experience. While their contributions are important, they only know by observing the effects and by interpreting what they hear, see, or read. Other PTSD book authors are on the "inside" such as wives and a few men or women suffering from PTSD, but very few offer the experiences of a trained counselor who was diagnosed with severe PTSD. Mike, because of his counseling training, has been able to give voice to the ideas that we have read and has interpreted what the ideas mean inside the mind of the wounded service member. He has counseled military members with PTSD and he has lived with PTSD. His story and interpretations are the essence of this book as we give voice to the wounded in spirit who search for meaning and hope.

Post Traumatic Stress Disorder (PTSD)

Post Traumatic Stress Disorder (PTSD) "is a mental health condition that's triggered by a terrifying event—either experiencing it or witnessing it. Symptoms may include flashbacks, nightmares and severe anxiety, as well as uncontrollable thoughts about the event" (Post-traumatic Stress Disorder, 2015). Any person can experience PTSD if traumatization results from an event and the effects of that traumatization remain for a period of time. PTSD is the name professionals in the medical and psychological field use to define warriors who are finding more difficulty in their transitions from combat zones to home.

In this book, we use the term, "warrior," to signify those military personnel who have served in the combat zones. The term, "post," is a rather obvious reference that signifies a time period after a traumatic event(s) has occurred. "Trauma" is a key word within this name as it refers to one or more events that profoundly affect those people who experience the event. War is regarded as traumatic, but other events such as sexual assault, physical abuse, and many others are also considered traumatic.

For the purposes of this book, we are focusing only on war and its after-effects as traumatic. Researchers pursuing war related stress find that "traumatic events frequently call into question the existential and spiritual issues related to the meaning of life, self-worth, and the safety of life" (Drescher, Smith, & Foy, 2007, p. 295). The final word, "disorder," is one with which many scholars and researchers disagree. For example, Edward Tick, in *War and the Soul*, argues that PTSD is not a stress disorder, but is, instead, an identity disorder. Tick explains (2005):

> The diagnosis of anxiety disorder wrongly assumes a pathological distortion that we can treat or medicate back into normalcy. This misunderstanding denies the ultimate nature of the transformation, causing survivors and their families to feel frustrated and alienated and demonstrating our culture's denial of war's impact. "Who am I now?" may be the most difficult and important question the survivor must finally answer. This is why, from the psychological perspective, it is so important to recognize PTSD as an identity disorder. (p. 106)

The trauma that warriors experience in the combat zone is not easily contained in the "psychological disorder" category. Trauma's effects are much more extensive, affecting how warriors define themselves and how they relate to others. Families struggle to understand the changes that have occurred in warriors when they return home.

The struggle that warriors face when they return is, in a philosophical sense, an identity disorder which is an existential problem. The ultimate meaning of suffering and of life, the continual search for meanings to war experiences, and the attempts to understand God's position within war are complex issues that warriors face upon returning home. The current methods of approaching these issues are through mind and body. The third part of our humanity, the spiritual side, is often overlooked in our Western approaches. This absence of addressing the spiritual wound is leading many warriors to continue searching for hope and healing. With most approaches such as posttraumatic growth, warriors have two-thirds of their wound addressed. PTSD is "the result of the way war invades, wounds and transforms our spirit....Conventional models of medical and psychological functioning and therapeutics are not adequate to explain or treat such wounds" (Tick, 2005, pp. 1-2). Tick continues by explaining that while wars have been fought for many different reasons, "war is indeed universally traumatizing" (Tick, 2005, p. 3). Thus, any experience with war has the potential to traumatize the people involved.

Even though Tick accurately identifies the problem of avoiding spiritual issues, Tick misses the mark when he recommends to adopt and adapt Native American rituals for healing. As Christians, we believe that no need exists to go outside the boundaries of the Christian faith. Our response is to approach our God through whom life is given. The ultimate question is "Who am I *now* in relation to God?" Walter Brueggemann addresses this situation in his study of the Psalms. He presents the concepts of orientation, disorientation, and new orientation. Thus, people have an understanding of an orientation for their lives which trauma disrupts. This disruption produces a time of disorientation that causes people to question the beliefs they held during the orientation period. Responses to disorientation can produce a new orientation (distinct from "new normal") to God, the world, and our families (Brueggemann, 2002, p. x). Through Brueggemann's ideas, we will present a journey to healing that is grounded in the Christian faith.

Trauma: Trauma and long term exposure to traumatic events that warriors experience in the combat zones can lead to diagnoses of PTSD, but this diagnosis is not automatic for returning warriors. The reasons why some people develop PTSD and others do not are not, at this time, fully understood. The fact that war changes our men and women who fight, however, is a fact. Charles Hoge (2010) explains the gap that exists between our culture in the U.S. and the returning warriors: "Society hasn't yet grasped that 'transitioning' home from combat does not mean giving up being a warrior, but rather learning to dial up or down the warrior responses depending on the situation" (p. x). Experiencing trauma causes people to face unspeakable atrocities and then attempt to make meaning from those traumatic experiences.

Judith Herman (1997) in her seminal book, *Trauma and Recovery*, explains how humans tend to respond to unspeakable atrocities. She argues that even though people try to bury the trauma, "The ordinary response to atrocities is to banish them from consciousness. Certain violations of the social compact are too terrible to utter aloud: this is the meaning of the word *unspeakable*" (p. 1). The smells, sounds, sights, and terrors visit warriors in their sleep and also in their waking hours. The experiences of warriors in the combat zone are not easily dismissed because of the horrors associated with them.

> Atrocities, however, refuse to be buried. Equally as powerful as the desire to deny atrocities is the conviction that denial does not work…Remembering and telling the truth about terrible events are prerequisites both for the restoration of the social order and for the healing of individual victims. The conflict between the will to deny horrible events and the will to proclaim them aloud is the central dialectic of psychological trauma. (Herman, 1997, p. 1)

Struggling to forget their experiences in the combat zone is a pointless activity for warriors. These horrors continue to plague them in nightmares and flashbacks until they find a way to express their traumatic experiences.

In describing his experiences in Vietnam, Karl Marlantes discusses the concept of sacred spaces in combat. While most people think of sacred space as a "light-filled wondrous place where we can feel good and find a way to shore up our psyches against death," warriors and those exposed to such horrors know that "something as ugly and brutal as combat" can also represent spiritual sacred spaces (Marlantes, 2011, p. 8). Knowledge of the differences between the "light" and the "dark" spiritual spaces can set warriors on the outside of the society to which they return after their combat tours. This gap can have "serious psychological and behavioral consequences" for the returning warriors. In order to avoid or lessen these consequences, "warriors have to be able to bring meaning to this chaotic experience, i.e., an understanding of their situation at a deeper level than proficiency in killing" (Marlantes, 2011, p. 8). Finding meaning within the horrific experiences of war is a spiritual search.

Marlantes continues with his analysis of the returning warrior: "There is also a deeper side to coming home. The returning warrior needs to heal more than his mind and body. He needs to heal his soul" (2011, p. 196). Healing of the spirit (soul) requires warriors to be able to find meaning in their experiences. Finding meaning in life is a spiritual quest. Warriors returning home seeking relief from PTSD must deal with the psychological and mental after-effects, but they must also face their spiritual trauma resulting from their exposure to war.

Posttraumatic Growth (PTG) and Spiritual Health

A major battle for traumatized warriors is the lack of understanding of their trauma by our Western culture. People often assume that "their lives are safe, predictable, and controllable" (Calhoun & Tedeschi, 2013, p. 128). Trauma changes all of these assumptions and warriors back from the combat zone with new understandings make people uncomfortable. Lawrence Calhoun and Richard Tedeschi conducted research with people who had experienced traumatic events. They, like other researchers, began to find that some people experienced growth because of their responses to the traumatic incident. "The emotional power of trauma can be a catalyst for deep processing that can yield beneficial new perspectives," (Calhoun & Tedeschi, 2013, p. 69). For most people, deep processing requires assistance from another person(s).

Tedeschi and Calhoun (2004) continue with their analysis of reactions to trauma:

> [T]he frightening and confusing aftermath of trauma, where fundamental assumptions are severely challenged, can be fertile ground for unexpected outcomes that can be observed in survivors: posttraumatic growth. The term *posttraumatic growth* refers to positive psychological change experienced as a result of the struggle with highly challenging life circumstances. (p. 1)

PTG refers to positive psychological changes in the traumatized individual which can lead these individuals to feeling that they have grown because of their traumatic experience.

In this book, we will expand the concept of "posttraumatic growth" that seeks positive psychological changes by developing the spiritual side of the wound that warriors receive in the combat zone. We live in a society whose members seek to be psychologically stable and physically fit with little to no concern about spiritual health. While God is concerned with every aspect of our life, God's concern lies more with our spiritual health than with our psychological stability or physical fitness. While not attempting to negate the need for psychoanalytic approaches, we are advocating the need for a strong Christian spirituality in the current approaches to PTSD treatments. In this book, we will use the terms, "Christian spirituality" and "spirituality," to be synonymous. Christian spirituality focuses on the spirit within us that responds to the call of the Holy Spirit to seek God through

His Son, Jesus Christ. It includes our seeking to understand the meaning of events in our lives, particularly traumatic events, in relationship to God through His Son, Jesus Christ. The seeking of that which can't be fully known, but must be accepted in faith is a part of Christian spirituality.

In the late 1990s, Mike brought a book home (to Iceland) from a conference in the U.S. This book, Robert Grant's *The Way of the Wound*, was instrumental in my spiritual journey at the time. Grant, a trauma specialist who has worked throughout the world, writes a book about healing the spiritual wounds that are the result of trauma. (His spelling choices are standard British English.) He explores how trauma is one of the last areas where the Holy Spirit can reach us. Through trauma, we can learn to live our lives as authentically as Jesus led His. This journey requires a difficult path that includes total submission to God.

One day as I stood in our library scanning the books, Grant's book jumped out at me. Now, I know that the Holy Spirit directed me to the book. At the time, I tried to remember what was in the book and decided to read it again to try to find some kind of help. As a result, we use *The Way of the Wound* to develop the narrative of how our family moved from Mike's return from three years of war through his PTSD diagnosis to the changes we instigated in our home and lives that then led to a spiritual journey that brought our family again to a place of peace and healing. Grant comments:

> Today's men and women are in desperate need of a spirituality that addresses the most dangerous aspects of life. Every victim of trauma knows these parts of life first hand. Those affected by war, murder, terrorism, spousal and child abuse, rape, violent crime, workplace violence and ecological devastation need a spirituality grounded in the hard realities of everyday living. Ultimately, spiritual meaning must emerge from the life-world and not from concepts or fear. (1996, p. x)

We have found healing through finding spiritual meaning in the wounds with which Mike returned from war. The journey has been a long road, but we have found our way to peace, hope, and spiritual healing. Our book is our journey to understanding PTSD and then to deepening our relationship with God. The journey we share is a sacred one. We share our story so that others may find the path to peace, hope, and spiritual healing.

What we bring to the PTSD/PTG discussion is our story—one that begins in the mire of a household where PTSD symptoms are in control but slowly journeys to being a household filled with hope and peace. We have found a way to bring peace and hope to Mike which, in turn, has restored peace and hope in our family. We laugh and tease as a family again. There is no magical cure. There is no pill that will cure this hidden wound. There is no quick fix. There is, however, a journey of the spirit that can bring peace and hope to the wounded. We have found that our Eternal Father *is* strong to save. His arm has bound the restless waves that pounded our household for several years.

Mike's war experiences ministering to warriors in combat zones have allowed him first-hand insights into the challenges of PTSD and the shame that accompanies diagnosis. However, his commitment to military members and his search for an authentic faith that produces an authentic ministry have led us to write this book. Henri Nouwen (1972) expresses our commitment to sharing our journey into a deeper authentic faith in *The Wounded Healer: Ministry in a Contemporary Society*:

> When the imitation of Christ does not mean to live a life like Christ, but to live your life as authentically as Christ lived his, then there are many ways and forms in which a man can be a Christian. The minister is the one who can make this search for authenticity possible, not by standing on the side as a neutral screen or an impartial observer, but as an articulate witness of Christ, who puts his own search at the disposal of others. (p. 99)

With these words, we put our own search at the disposal of others who are seeking an authentic faith that can encompass the traumas of war and its aftermath.

The Navy Hymn as a Framework

We are a Navy family that has at our core a deep faith in God. In chapels at Camp Lejeune; Marine Corps Air Stations (Cherry Point and New River); Naval Station Pearl Harbor; Naval Air Station Keflavik, Iceland; Naval Station Newport, Rhode Island; and many other places, we have sung the Navy hymn, *Eternal Father, Strong to Save*. As we subdivided our journey into and through this hidden wound, it seemed natural that we would use a nautical framework. The Navy hymn also reminds us that it is through the storms and rough seas that God, Christ, and the Holy Spirit guide us. Thus, our chapters reflect the spiritual journey that the entirety of the Navy hymn, with its many verses, lays out for those in earlier days as well as today. Faith is a core part of the journey through this wound. Each of the chapter titles and the names of the chapters below come from the William Whiting's (1860) song, "Eternal Father, Strong to Save." We used one additional verse by Hugh Taylor (n. d.).

I begin our story in Chapter 2 with the "before time" of the first twenty years of our marriage so we can share how our family changed when Mike returned with an invisible wound. "Protect the Ones We Love at Home" reflects thirty-six years of Mike's military service and twenty-five years of our family's Navy experiences. Our purpose is not to share anger or to obtain pity, but we want to establish who we were, so that we can express how our family changed when Mike returned from the war. In explaining our relationship, we then can explain our journey through PTSD to spiritual health. "O Hear Us When We Cry to Thee" is the title of Chapter 3. I continue in this chapter by explaining how PTSD made itself known in our home. Our family's cries and Mike's cries to God were many and frequent as our communication and family broke down.

"For Those in Peril on the Sea," Chapter 4, tells Mike's side of the story as he expresses his thoughts over the same period of time as Chapter 3. Comparing Chapters 3 and 4 conveys the distance between us when Mike came home. This chapter explains how Mike first admitted he might have some issues and then began counseling in Newport, RI. Chapter 5, "Our Brethren Shield in Danger's Hour," defines "trauma" from multiple aspects with the underlying concept of shielding those in the combat zone when they are in dangerous situations. Interwoven through this chapter are some of Mike's experiences and stories from Afghanistan and Iraq that will bring the definitions of trauma to life.

"Most Holy Spirit Who Didst Brood Upon the Chaos Dark and Rude," Chapter 6, is the beginning of my discovery of ways to assist Mike as he attempted to find relief from the chaos in his brain. This chapter contains discussions of what the warrior's behavior means to the family and what the warrior's behavior means in the combat zone. The next chapter, Chapter 7 "And Bid Its Angry Tumult Cease," presents the methods that I employed in our home to accommodate Mike's needs. Understanding PTSD and changing my views on PTSD allowed me to employ several changes in our home to create a safe environment for Mike to journey toward spiritual healing.

The last chapters are Mike's story. Chapter 8 "And Hushed Their Raging at Thy Word" focuses on Mike's shame, guilt, and hopelessness. As he sought help through another year of counseling, Mike found his mind and body improving. His spirit, however, was still deeply wounded. The chaos began to settle, but it was still controlling Mike's spirit. The spiritual journey Mike began as a response to the changes I made in the home is the story of Chapter 9 "Protect Them Wheresoe'er They Go." The rigorous journey requires total submission to the Holy Spirit. This submission is difficult for warriors who have used control and self-protection to survive in the combat zone. Mike eventually took the journey through his wound and found, on the other side, that he had a deeper knowledge of and faith in God. Through this experience, Mike found spiritual healing. Our last chapter, Chapter 10 "And Give, for Wild Confusion, Peace," summarizes the concepts that we have presented in the book. We also offer some challenges to our readers and to those who want to help relieve the agony and pain of traumatized warriors. Most of all, we offer a way to discover hope and peace for the traumatized spirit.

Our story is one of hope. Mike has traveled this path. We do not live in a fairy tale land where life has no difficulties, but we do live with the reality that Mike has experienced a wound that will be with him for life. He, however, has found a way to calm the wild confusion in his mind. He is able to hope again and he has come to a place where he can experience peace again. This story of spiritual healing from traumatic events is the story that we share. May God show you the way to Him through this writing.

An Added Note

I will close this chapter with a story that compares the extreme difference that has occurred in our family over the last ten years as Mike has attempted to find his way through his wound. We moved to Newport, Rhode Island, soon after Mike's return from the war. He had accepted the Commanding Officer billet at the Naval Chaplains School that was located at Naval Station, Newport, RI. The school was in the process of moving to Fort Jackson in Columbia, SC. This new responsibility required Mike to make multiple trips to Fort Jackson every month. When he would leave, our normally chaotic household would become a place of relative calm, even though we had three kids from ages twelve to twenty-two living with us. Several times when Mike was gone, our children would ask me, "Is it bad to say that I'm glad that Daddy isn't home right now?" I would tell them that they could feel that way but to remember that their dad had experienced a wound from the war. I bore the guilt of also being glad for a bit of calmness in between storms.

Recently, Mike went to Germany for seven weeks. Even though two of our children are in college twenty miles away, they both called me and said, "I really miss Dad. When will he be home?" They told me they miss going to lunch and interacting with him once a week—a habit they started this year. They have even come home, only to say that it seems empty and lonely without their father home.

That is the reason that we are sharing our story. Mike has walked through the way of the wound and has found his way to a spiritual health that allows him not to be controlled by his PTSD symptoms. The results are that we miss him and want him home again when he leaves. Those families with a member who has this PTSD wound understand the tremendous growth that Mike has done. When the kids miss their father and want him home—and I want my husband home—that says enough for the story we have to tell. Our life is not perfect but PTSD is a wound Mike has accepted as part of who he is, but not as the controller of his life. In this journey, Mike has found that God is once again the Lord of his life.

CHAPTER TWO

"Protect the Ones We Love at Home"

During our marriage, Mike spent over nine years away from home with the Navy. Of the twenty-five years we were married and he was in the Navy, Mike was away thirty-five percent of the time. The necessity of caring for our family and maintaining our home fell on me, since he was away so often. I accepted and enjoyed the responsibilities as well as the opportunities to make a difference in our commands. Mike retired in 2011 as the Commanding Officer for the Naval Chaplaincy School and Center. The path to that retirement, however, was one filled with adventures and struggles as we grew stronger and stronger in our commitment to each other, to our family, and to God.

Mike and I met in October 1984 when we were both working on our Master of Divinity degrees at Southeastern Theological Seminary in Wake Forest, NC. Mike was thirty and I was twenty-six. We both had experienced full lives before meeting each other. I was a post-Vietnam anti-military liberal who embraced intellectualism as the best way to encounter the world. I considered myself rather worldly because I read a lot. At the time I met Mike, I had hardly left the four state region of South Carolina, North Carolina, Georgia, and Tennessee. I had never been overseas, but had visited the Grand Canyon and Boston. Mike's life up to that point had been quite different.

Mike's life experiences incorporated worldwide trips through football and the Marine Corps. At the University of Louisiana at Lafayette, Mike had played college football (offensive guard) throughout his college career. Traveling to games with the Ragin' Cajuns took him all over the United States and to Hawaii. Entering the Marine Corps' Platoon Leader Class, Mike started his military duty the summer before his junior year when he attended the first half of Officer Candidate School (OCS). He completed the second half of his training in the summer before his senior year and then went to The Basic School in Quantico, VA, in January 1978. In retrospect, Mike's military career was interwoven with the politics of the Middle East.

U.S. Marine Corps Infantry Officer

As a new Second Lieutenant, Mike was stationed in Okinawa for a year. During this time, Mike became a global citizen, tasting any food he could and experiencing the culture of Okinawa, mainland Japan, Philippines, and Korea as much as possible. He traveled throughout the countries and hiked with a full pack through a great deal of the countryside. At that time, Marines in Okinawa provided support, as needed, throughout all of Asia and also in the Middle East.

On 14 February 1979, the U.S. ambassador to Afghanistan, Adolph Dubs, was kidnapped by terrorists while being driven to work. He was held for several hours in a hotel room in Kabul before being killed in a botched rescue attempt. Mike's Marine unit was tapped to fly into Kabul, Afghanistan, to provide assistance and security for the embassy personnel who were going to be evacuated. Mike's unit was on the tarmac for several hours, waiting for the "Go" order to come from Jimmy Carter's government. The order never came so the Marines reluctantly stood down. No show of force was done at the embassy. On 9 November 1979—a few months later—militants overran the U.S. Embassy in Tehran, Iran, which resulted in more than sixty embassy personnel being held hostage for 444 days. This experience was Mike's first time standing on the edge of history. It also was the first of his many encounters with hostilities in the Middle East.

After his tour in Okinawa, Mike was stationed at Quantico, VA, at The Basic School as an instructor. His duties included teaching physical fitness, patrolling, tactics, hand-to-hand combat skills, and land navigation to men and women wanting to be Marine officers. During this time, Mike played rugby and enjoyed the life of a young man with a salary and no family responsibilities. After a few wild times that included having roommates burn down the house they lived in, Mike found a church to attend and began to feel that God was calling him to something more.

In 1983, Mike decided to attend seminary to begin studying theology. When the General saw Mike's resignation papers, he called Mike to his office. He told Mike that he was in the process of recommending him to be assigned to 2nd Marine Corps Reconnaissance Battalion at Camp Lejeune, NC, and asked Mike to stay in the Marines. One of Mike's dreams had been to become a part of the Recon units so the offer was tempting. Mike, however, decided to follow through with this new calling on his life to train for the chaplaincy. He turned down the offer and had several months to serve before his resignation became effective.

During that time, Mike had several friends who became part of the Recon units that he would have been assigned to. They completed their training and went to Beirut, Lebanon, as part of the Multinational Force that the UN sent to oversee the Lebanese civil war. On 23 October 1983, a group called "Islamic Jihad" drove two trucks to the Marine barracks where U.S. and French troops were housed. The explosion on the Marine Barracks killed 299 American and French military members. Of that total, 220 Marines, eighteen sailors, and three soldiers were killed. Of the remaining Americans, 128 Marines were injured with thirteen later dying of their wounds.

Mike lost his friends that day. This second encounter with the Middle East brought a more personal tragedy to Mike. The realization that he would have been there or possibly Grenada for that landing if he had joined Recon was a sobering thought.

Mike began seminary in January 1984. I had begun a semester before him. We were in a class together and mutual friends introduced us. We became best friends over the next few months. We met in October 1984, became engaged in November, and married in May 1985. Mike remained in the U.S. Marine Corps Reserves during this time.

After our graduation from seminary, Mike had to serve two years in a ministry role in order to gain the experience that the Navy required for chaplains. We moved first to Columbia, SC, where Mike spent a year in Clinical Pastoral Education (CPE), an internship program for hospital chaplains. Our first child, Michael, Jr., was born while we were in Columbia. Next, we moved to a community outside of Brevard, NC, where Mike served as a pastor to a small church for his second year of experience.

Mike pastored the church while I was in charge of religious education. This division of labor was to become the norm for us in Mike's chapels. While we were in Brevard, we hiked the surrounding mountains many weekends. Mike took his daily five-mile runs through the farms that bordered the French Broad River and I canned food for the first and last time. We lived near enough to family that Michael, Jr., formed a deep bound with his grandparents. Mike transitioned from the Marine Corps to the Navy during our time in Brevard.

U.S. Navy Chaplain

Mike resigned his commission in the U.S. Marine Corps in November 1987, and was sworn in as a Lieutenant in the U.S. Navy in November 1987. Mike spent January through March 1988 in the Naval Chaplains School course aboard Naval Station Newport, RI, that was the staff officer's Officer Candidate School. Upon completion of the course in March 1988, Mike was told that he would have to wait five years to be able to move to active duty. However, three months later, we began our active duty experience.

MCAS New River, NC: Mike's first billet (job) with the military as a chaplain was with Marine Aircraft Group 29 (MAG 29) at MCAS New River. Mike traveled often; some, because of assignment and some, because of volunteering. Mike worked two jobs while at MCAS New River: MAG 29 from July 1988 through January 1990 and Marine Wing Support Group (MWSG) 27 which covered four squadrons: Marine Wing Support Squadron (MWSS) 271 at MCAS Cherry Point, NC; MWSS 272 at MCAS New River; MWSS 273 at MCAS Beaufort, SC; and MWSS 274 at Bogue Field, NC from Jan 1990 through June 1991. These jobs provided Mike many opportunities to travel throughout the U.S. and the world with different squadrons.

Mike routinely went to Cold Weather Training in Wisconsin and Norway. He was part of a MARTIME pre-position of ships that performed a strategic offload in Honduras from April through May of 1990. He also participated in a variety of trainings and was selected for several TAD (Temporary Additional Duty) that found him away from home more often than he was home.

My first experience with military members outside of the neighborhood and church came with my first job. I taught religion courses aboard MCAS New River for a university. My post-Vietnam images of the military were shattered by having classes full of uniforms and boots as Marines filled my classes. As I began to understand the military more and more through exposure to my students as well as regular lessons from my husband, I found my previous prejudices about the military falling away and being replaced by a deep respect for the men and women who join the Marine Corps. I became very active in spouse groups where I found a great opportunity to assist young wives who had no idea how to survive when their husband was deployed. I became the Key Wife representative for MWSS 272 at MCAS New River in January 1990.

Mike's comings and goings greatly contrasted with my upbringing where my father, a doctor, was home every night for dinner. We lived a very predictable life—always vacationing for two weeks in the summer on Hilton Head Island, SC, and enjoying the fall leaves for a weekend in October in Gatlinburg, TN. My father came home as late as 9 p.m. during flu season but he was always home for dinner. I was faced with raising my son in an environment that was unpredictable, but I soon learned to deal with absences.

I read many items on preparing for deployments and readjusting afterwards. Mike and I presented pre- and post-deployment workshops for families at MCAS New River as well as Marine Corps Base Camp Lejeune. We learned ways to cope with his comings and goings and soon, this way of living became the normal way our family lived.

Mike and I found that we had developed a very effective system for his deployments and his TAD times. I did, however, hold some resentment because I was "stuck" in Jacksonville, NC, while Mike was traveling the country and the world. When I finally shared this resentment with Mike, he looked at me in a confused way and said, "Kathy, do you think I really enjoy these places when you two aren't with me? Yes, I do enjoy seeing the new places but I am always thinking of what I will show to you when I bring you back to that place." After that, I realized that my jealousy of his wonderful times was misplaced. We said goodbye and hello so many times that we lost count. But each time, we readjusted with minimal problems because we would sit down and discuss whatever was bothering us. Our friendship deepened and our marriage bonds strengthened each time Mike returned home.

Desert Shield/Desert Storm: In the summer of 1990, Mike began preparations to deploy with MWSS 271 (MCAS Cherry Point) to Europe for two months in the fall. They would complete training in several parts of Europe, including Norway where Mike had already been twice. Mike was excited about the aspect of returning to the area. He had conducted services in the caves in Norway's fjords where Hitler had hidden weapons.

However on 2 August 1990, these plans changed when Saddam Hussein invaded Kuwait. The group of Marines scheduled to deploy to Europe were rapidly renamed "Marine Aircraft Group (MAG) 40" and were placed on ships which sailed from Moorehead City, NC, on 5 August 1990. Mike found himself wedged aboard USS *Guam* (LPH 9) with the Marines who had been scheduled to go to Europe as well as Marines from other commands.

I wrote Mike every day and sent many packages to him. By this time, all of America was "proud to be an American" and was answering the call to send mail to "any sailor." Americans sent so many packages and so much mail that family mail did not get through to the sailors and Marines very rapidly. Mike received his first letter from me in early October with no other letter until the ship pulled into port in Dubai, United Arab Emirates, on the week before Thanksgiving. I received one letter in early October but nothing else between August and November until that first phone call on the day before Thanksgiving.

Mike was able to call at Christmas as well but, other than that, our communication centered on "snail mail" letters delivered in large batches about once a month. There were also MARS grams (twenty-five word messages sent by short wave radio operators throughout the world) available, but they were generally used for important matters (like announcements of moving to another duty station). During this time, Mike ministered to the Marines aboard *Guam* that was floating in the Persian Gulf as a threatening landing force in Kuwait. He conducted services, baptized new believers, and counseled Marines as they waited aboard *Guam*.

As time passed and Saddam Hussein continued to defy the United Nations directives, planning for an assault became more and more of a reality. MAG 40 was part of the Marine Expeditionary Brigade that consisted of infantry Marines who were planning an amphibious assault on the beaches just south of the Kuwaiti airport. The chaplain assigned to these Marines refused to accompany them in a landing if they went. His refusal caused him to be moved to another section that would not make the landing. Mike volunteered to replace him and accompany the Marines who would wade through the land mines that filled the Kuwaiti coast. Mike's concern was primarily for the spiritual needs of the landing force.

Operation Desert Shield became Operation Desert Storm on 17 January 1991, when the ground forces began to take back Kuwait and the other areas that Saddam Hussein had claimed. On two occasions during that week, Iraqi aircraft attacked *Guam* during the night, causing *Guam* to go to General Quarters. The U.S. and other countries rolled through Iraq so that a landing was not necessary. Thus, Mike and the Marines stayed aboard the ships.

During this time, I was the Key Wife coordinator for MWSS 272. (Each branch of the military has spouses that provide support for the families in deployed units. In the early 1990s, the Marine Corps used Key Wives and the Navy used Ombudsmen.) Mike was the only person deployed from the area in August, but by January, most of Jacksonville had deployed. As the Key Wife coordinator, I assisted the spouses with issues they might face in their daily lives. I knew most of the resources in the area and found my "niche" in supplying the needed information to help with problems as they arose. We filmed family messages to send to the unit and we scheduled events to help families cope with deployment. I continued to teach throughout this time, though my classes were very small because the Marines and sailors were deployed.

After the war itself ended, *Guam* stayed in the Persian Gulf area until May 1991 when it set sail for home. Stopping in Israel for a port call before crossing the Atlantic provided Mike the opportunity to baptize men in the Jordan River. Mike was also able to tour the Holy Land of Israel before returning home.

Arriving home at the end of May 1991, Mike hitched a ride with Marines returning to MCAS New River in helicopters. Michael and I watched for Mike as he came off one of the twelve helicopters that landed. They all were in desert khakis, looked the same in the lines, and marched the same way as they approached the families. Mike found us before we found him.

Our readjustment went smoothly though the move overshadowed most of the readjustment. We were living in a different place than when Mike left; but overall, he fit in and we were back to our regular family routines. While I had taught the post-deployment workshops for spouses aboard MCAS New River, Mike had taught the Marines and sailors returning with him. Our adjustment had a few arguments, but overall, we were excited at the aspect of shore duty so that we could be together more. Our friendship continued to grow through this time and our marriage strengthened. Our faith had strengthened as each of us served God in the places and positions in which He placed us.

We ended our tour at MCAS New River with an expertise in pre- and post-deployment training, excellent skills for coping with deployments, and a renewed friendship. The hardest part of separation, we both agreed, was not having our best friend to talk to. In hindsight, we saw our marriage commitment to each other strengthened by the deployments.

Mike's third encounter with the Middle East, first actual trip to the Middle East, and first war experience ended with his return. He had orders for our move to Naval Air Station Cubi Point in the Philippines. We lined up the move, sold our van, and left the area in two weeks. We planned to drive to the port in Los Angeles to ship our car so that we could visit family across the U.S. on our way. We arrived in Houston, TX, to the news that Mount Pinatubo in the Philippines was erupting. The volcano was dumping tremendous amounts of ash and other elements on Clark Air Force Base, Naval Station Subic Bay, and Naval Air Station Cubi Point. Because they were evacuating these bases, our travel orders were cancelled and we reported to the nearest Naval Base—Corpus Christi Naval Air Station in Texas. After three weeks, Mike was assigned to USS *Chosin* (CG-65), a brand new Aegis guided missile cruiser, in Pearl Harbor, Hawaii. We headed out for back-to-back operational tours, with this one being sea duty. "Hawaii," however, made the back-to-back tours much more tolerable.

USS Chosin *(CG 65) Pearl Harbor, Hawaii:* We arrived in a bright, open airport that smelled of flowers. We were greeted by our sponsors and told that because our orders were changed so abruptly, housing had not been arranged for us. We would have to stay in a hotel until a house opened. Our sponsors had made reservations for us in a hotel one block from Waikiki Beach.

Mike reported to *Chosin* in June 1991. This brand new ship was part of the USS *Ranger* (CV-61) Battle Group which was home ported in San Diego, CA. When we arrived, *Chosin* was beginning preparations for a WestPAC deployment. Over the next few months, the ship traveled to San Diego to join *Ranger* and the rest of the battle group as they completed the work ups for deployment. Instead of the normal time at sea, *Chosin* was able to add on the travel time to and from San Diego to that normal time so our separations were longer than the rest of the battle group. We began another tour with Mike's absences outnumbering his days in port.

Our first December in Hawaii occurred on the celebration of the 50th anniversary of the bombing of Pearl Harbor. Veterans flew in from all over the United States and spent a week or more on Oahu. We went to a survivor's parade in downtown Honolulu. *Chosin* was selected to render colors as it passed USS *Arizona* on 7 December 1991. Mike offered the prayer as *Chosin* came abreast of *Arizona* while giving honors as she passed in review.

We listened to the stories that the men and women who returned to Hawaii fifty years after the bombing told us. We listened to the men tell of the tap—tap—tap that they heard standing guard at USS *Utah* when it ran aground. One man told us how many days, hours, and minutes that they listened to the taps of men who would never be reached. They waited hours for the next tap that never came. Another man told us of his five first-wave landings with the Marines on Guadalcanal, Iwo Jima, Tarawa, and other islands. He lost four brothers on four islands, but he had lived to come back fifty years later. As I listened to more and more stories, I came to understand that time does not heal all wounds. Some wounds are too deep for healing.

Mike left for a six-month WestPAC deployment in 1992, returning to the Persian Gulf less than a year after leaving it. *Chosin* traveled across the Pacific by way of Hong Kong, Singapore, Thailand, and other countries. This trip completed Mike's circling the earth. When they returned, the ship visited several ports including Perth, Sydney, and Townville, Australia. They also made port calls at Tarawa and Kwajalein Atoll before coming home in February 1993. While he was deployed, I was an active member of the Spouse Club, offering support where I could. I worked as an elementary school teacher for the first and last time during this time as well.

On 9 December 1993, our second son, Jeff, was born. We left Hawaii on 18 December 1993 for Yorktown, VA. Two back-to-back operational tours had been costly to us emotionally, but we developed a stronger marriage which surprised us. We had kept God at the center of our marriage and remained committed to each other and our friendship. This pattern proved successful for us through the long separations and through wartime.

NWS Yorktown, VA: We moved to Virginia in January 1994, where Mike was the Command Chaplain for Naval Weapons Station (NWS) Yorktown. He took over the chapel aboard Naval Weapons Station Yorktown. He was the only chaplain at this command and our first Sunday in services revealed that we also were the only people attending the Protestant worship service. Mike's first Sunday in the pulpit found the pews filled with our two sons, me, and the organist when she was not playing music. Over the next two and a half years, Mike grew the chapel from five attendees to over eighty-five regular attendees in the Sunday services.

We bought a house and learned to enjoy military life with Mike home. I helped with the religious education in the chapel, including teaching a woman's Bible study. Mike held services, began Bible studies, and counseled many couples and single adults. He grew a congregation that filled the church. We made neighborhood friends, and found that our marriage and friendship had endured the long absences of our early years. Mike was also able to complete his Doctor of Ministry degree during this tour.

After two and one-half years in Virginia, Mike received orders to move to another chapel. This time, we would move to Naval Air Station, Keflavik, Iceland, so that Mike could minister in the base chapel there. We left Virginia in October 1996 with ten-year old Michael, two-year-old Jeff, and three-month-old Elizabeth.

NAS Keflavik, Iceland: The plane stopped at the terminal and a set of stairs was placed outside the plane for the passengers to exit. As we left the plane that morning of 5 October 1996, the wind blew the baby carrier sideways and the snow pelted us. I yelled at Mike to grab Jeff as the wind blew him down. Mike turned around, picked Jeff up, and grabbed my arm to usher us into the terminal. Elizabeth, at three-months-old, had the shocked look of the baby that cannot breathe in the wind. Michael ran inside after he caught the baby blanket that blew away from us. After an all night flight with a fussy baby, I was not sure what had just happened.

Our sponsors met us in the terminal after we went through customs. I looked around the bleak, barren terminal with a vague memory of flower scented air and openness that had greeted us when we had flown across a different ocean. As we drove to our quarters, I was struck most by the bleakness of the base. The housing had rocks and grass. There were no trees or flowers or anything to bring beauty to the barrenness.

Mike began his chapel duties and found that the base hospital was also part of his duties. We settled in and, after awhile, learned to enjoy the subtle differences in the days and nights, in the lava fields, and in the country. I worked as the Religious Education Director planning events, organizing Sunday School, etc. I also worked with spouse groups. We lived in Iceland for four years, leaving in June 2000. Our last flight out was a sad one, but we were returning to Jacksonville, NC, where we had lived before.

Camp Lejeune, NC: We moved back to Jacksonville, NC, in August 2000 for Mike to begin his tour as the Deputy Command Chaplain for 2D Marine Division at Camp Lejeune, NC. Mike traveled a bit and went for two-week deployments in various places, but most of his duties kept him home. I began teaching for the same university that I had taught with before which allowed me to gain a deeper understanding of Marines and sailors than I had had before.

We had just begun our second year when our country was attacked on 11 September 2001. Mike did not have to leave this time because he was the Deputy Chaplain. Our lives were changed by that attack and how we did business on base and off changed as well. We formed more extensive networks for our children in case they were on base and we were off or vice versa. The safety net became more and more complex. We saw many friends off to war and I waited for Mike to volunteer. He received new orders before that time came.

NS Newport, RI: In May 2002, I received my Master of Arts degree from East Carolina University shortly before the packers showed up in June 2002, to move us to Newport, RI. Mike had been selected to attend the Naval War College Senior Course where, over the next year, he received his second Masters degree.

When Mike's year at the Naval War College ended, he moved to the Naval Chaplains School (also in Newport) as the Advanced Course Officer. During this year, we had one of the worst winters that Newport had seen in awhile. When Mike was offered orders to Virginia, we decided that it was time to move to a warmer climate. While we were in Rhode Island, I was able to teach for two universities while also beginning my Doctor of Philosophy (PhD) degree in English. I completed all of my coursework and was ready to begin my oral exams when we received new orders. Little did I know at the time that I would not complete the degree for seven more years due to wars and other challenges.

NS Norfolk, VA: We left Newport, RI, in June 2004. Mike's new position was to require tremendous travel so we made the decision for him to live in the Norfolk area during the week and drive to North Carolina on the weekends. Mike began setting up a new way to assign chaplains to commands, the Operational Ministry Center. He was to have set up the Norfolk area, then San Diego, and continue through the major fleet centers in the U.S. The plan, however, began to change because of political interference and kept changing until the job was difficult to define.

Frustrated with the politics, Mike volunteered to go to Afghanistan as the Theater Chaplain. He called me to tell me that he had volunteered to do a six-month tour in Afghanistan and that he had two weeks before he left. The moment of shock that I felt was quickly replaced with the practical question of what can I help with? We made lists and began to complete them in high gear.

CFC-A Kabul, Afghanistan: Mike left for the Combined Forces Command (CFC-A) in Kabul, Afghanistan, on 5 August 2005 for a six-month tour. This six-month tour turned into an eleven-month tour so that Mike could accomplish what he needed to before returning home. The afternoon before Mike left, Michael, Jeff, Elizabeth, and I stood crowded together as Mike took the oath of office and pinned on his Eagles as a Navy Captain. We all clapped. Then we ran to the Exchange before it closed, grabbed some dinner, and tried to slow the clock down.

Mike said goodbye to us as he entered the terminal. We stood as a family—Michael (19), Jeff (11), and Elizabeth (9)—until Mike said, "I have to go now." We all smiled and waved goodbye with the kids yelling goofy things at Mike and holding up an "L" shape with their hands. Mike turned around, gave the kids a big "L" for "losers" (their latest joke), blew kisses at us, yelled, "I love you," and went into the terminal. I did not know, at the time, that I was telling my husband goodbye forever. I did not know that I would never see that man who left us that day again. If I had known, I am not sure what I would have done differently, but hugging a bit tighter and holding on a bit longer might have been part of it. Having him stay at home was not an option. It would be ten years before my husband would return from war.

For the next eleven months, Mike was over the NATO chaplains in the Afghan Theater. As the tensions rose, Mike was able to begin a relationship with Major General Amin Nasib, Chief of Religious and Cultural Affairs in the Afghan National Army. As their relationship grew, General Nasib expressed his approval of Mike's respect for the religion of the country. The inroads that Mike made with General Nasib was an early part of the Religious Leader Engagement approach that chaplains began to use as they approached the imams in Iraq and Afghanistan to communicate in ways that had not been possible when the military leaders had tried. The combination of military and religion that the chaplain's role encompassed gave the Afghani and Iraqi leaders a regard for our military that they had previously lacked.

In June 2006, Mike came home from the war in Afghanistan after spending eleven months in the combat zone. Reporting to Second Marine Division at Camp Lejeune, NC, he was scheduled to deploy to Fallujah, Iraq, in January 2007. My expectations of Mike during this time period were minimal. From our deployments early in our career, I knew that he was not able to be completely home. Returning to war in six months meant that a part of Mike never really returned home. From our first two operational tours, I had learned that military members form a certain mindset when they leave home. If they return for a short period of time, they just remain in that mindset instead of reintegrating into home life. Even though I wanted Mike to be his "old" self, I knew that he was not able to do so because he was going back so soon.

2D Marine Division was fully into war preparations; thus, Mike came home from the war in Afghanistan to war preparations for Iraq. I accepted that he was not as engaging because of his rapid turnaround. I found reasons to rationalize Mike's behavior because we had been through similar turnarounds when he was aboard *Chosin*. For my part, I decided to pretend that all was well and there was no war for Mike to return to.

One fall Saturday afternoon, Mike and I were sitting on the back porch while I updated Mike on the kids and told him about a new type of gear that the boys wanted for football season. The product was expensive, but both boys insisted that they needed this new compression gear called "Under Armour."

When I mentioned the name, Mike sat up straight and said, "NO. They will NOT wear that gear. I don't want my sons in Under Armour." Mike was adamant about his refusal and I was confused. I pressed him on why he was so against the gear. He refused to answer and said, "Just don't let them get it. Promise me….you won't get it for them, will you?"

Confused, I promised and let the issue rest. That new electronic toy that Mike had brought home dinged again. Mike looked at it and then attached his new Blackberry to his belt. We silently rocked and felt the breeze. After a few minutes, the Blackberry dinged again.

"What is that and why is it making that dinging noise?" I asked.

"It's called a Blackberry. I get messages on it and it dings when an update goes out. I am receiving messages about the casualties that are happening with the Marines."

"Now? Right now they are fighting and dying?" I asked.

"Yes," Mike answered tersely.

I sat back stunned. The pleasant afternoon seemed to be stolen from the young Marines who were dying in Iraq while I sat on my porch, enjoying the breeze. Each time Mike's Blackberry went "ding," I was overwhelmed with sadness for those who were fighting while America enjoyed carefree Saturday afternoons.

When we were ready to go in, I stopped Mike and said, "I will not buy the gear for the boys, but why are you so opposed to Under Armour. I had never heard of it until they asked for it recently."

Mike pulled out his Blackberry and held it up for me to see. "These Marines...you don't know what happens. I saw it a lot in Afghanistan. You don't know what Under Armour does."

"What does it do? Does it cut their circulation or something?" I couldn't imagine anything more than that.

"No, when an IED explodes or when there is a fire, it melts on them," Mike said, still holding his Blackberry up to me.

"On their skin? It melts on their skin?" I stupidly asked, trying to absorb this additional level of horror.

"Yes. You can't imagine the smell and the screams of the Marines as the docs pull it off of them. You just can't imagine...." Mike's voice faded off and his eyes told me that he was halfway around the world.

Later, I would discuss the issue with Mike again and he would reluctantly agree to allow the boys to have the gear. At the time, I did not understand the depth of this trauma in my husband's spirit, but I could not figure out a way to tell the boys they could not have the gear because it might melt to them if they are near fire. Those glimpses of the horror of war have stayed with me every day since that Blackberry pinged throughout the afternoon and I learned what the "latest thing" for the young men on the football fields was doing to young men on the battlefield. I have not had the same sort of "carefree" Saturday since that day.

Camp Fallujah, Iraq: Thanksgiving turned into Christmas and with that, Mike was gone again. I was so tired when Mike left. I was working full-time and teaching on base in the evenings. The kids were in sports, including Taekwondo. Michael, our oldest, was in college nearby. I was tired before Mike came home from Afghanistan and I grew more and more tired as the day for his leaving approached.

We went with Mike to the busses at Camp Lejeune to watch him board. We were more somber at this farewell. I told the kids to smile. Our youngest was 10 and our oldest was 20. We smiled and hugged Mike, but could find few words beyond, "I love you," to say. Major battles had been occurring in and around Fallujah. Even our youngest knew the danger that Mike was going into. Mike hugged me tightly and said, "I'll be OK. Don't worry," and then he was gone.

We watched the busses leave. We waved. Then we walked to the car, got in, and left. I felt for tears but all I could feel was numbness. One of the kids said, "It's like Daddy wasn't even home." I agreed and told them again about duty, honor, and commitment. I explained again that their Dad answered the call that so many people no longer answer. Then we discussed what it means to commit your life to God.

The days began to drag by. When Mike arrived at Camp Fallujah, he was able to begin to call home, though the calls were sporadic. I worked and cared for the kids. I never seemed to get enough sleep. As the weeks passed, Mike was able to call more. Often, the calls were late at night. I would be so tired but felt that I had to talk to him. The more we talked, the angrier he would become and, in return, the angrier I would become. I found myself wishing for the days before the Internet and before constant phone calls.

I became more and more numb as each day passed. During February 2007, I began a cycle having a major issue happen every two weeks or so. My purse was stolen with my IDs and credit cards. I had to figure out how to replace the IDs and other lost documents. I lost my wedding ring because it was in my purse. My hands had been swelling so much that I could not wear my ring very much.

Two weeks later, my sister called to tell me her cancer had returned. I began to drive back and forth to Greenville on the weekends to help my Dad care for my sister. During this time, I became aware of how far my father's dementia had progressed.

Major incidents such as these continued to happen until I went to the doctor in May to find out why my hands were swollen, my body was so stiff, and I was so tired. I had developed rheumatoid arthritis. I had lost twenty to forty percent usage of each shoulder. I had difficulty moving my hands. I had always been a runner, but I had not been running because of the pain that was in my knees, ankles, and feet. When the doctor finished examining me, he determined that I had severe RA (rheumatoid arthritis) in all of my joints but my elbows.

The doctor recommended that I call my husband's command to have him brought home immediately. I told the doctor that Mike would be home in February 2008. The doctor insisted that I contact the command to have Mike brought home. I refused. He argued a bit more, but I was insistent that my husband was not coming home.

I did not tell Mike that I had rheumatoid arthritis for a month. I was on the medications and they had begun to work. Once I had positive news, I told him. The war was raging in the Al Anbar Province and Mike had concerns there. I didn't want to add to the weight he already carried until I could handle the idea myself.

I continued to grow more and more numb as the months went by. The summer was a bit of a blur with medications not working and watching the inflammation fill my joints. Knowing that the inflammation was eating my joints frightened me deeply. I wished that Mike could be there because he could always make my fears disappear. I knew, however, that what he was doing in Iraq was so much more important than what I needed. I had help and I had a great doctor. We just had to continue trying until we found the right drugs. Allergies and bad reactions narrowed the range down to two choices. I began to learn to live with pain, stiffness, and fatigue.

The fall moved toward Thanksgiving and I continued to have a major problem every two to three weeks. In September, I thought back over the time since Mike had left and all of the issues that had presented themselves…and suddenly, all of that changed from overwhelming to humorous. After all, who really has so many issues and problems when her husband deploys? I began to pray that God would strengthen me for what was to come. Before this, my prayer had been for God to remove what was happening or something similar. My attitude changed and I found myself in a deeper relationship with God.

Service members who spend twelve months or more in the combat zone are allowed two weeks of leave. They usually take this leave, called "mid-tour leave," close to the middle of their tours. Mike waited until everyone on his team had taken leave and returned to Iraq. Thus, Mike didn't come home for his mid-tour leave until the end of November (ten-months into his thirteen-month tour). He was, however, able to help decorate for Christmas, one of Mike's favorite activities. It was a hollow time. I did my best to hide my symptoms but it was impossible. I did, however, pretend to be much better than I was at the time. Mike angered easily, was restless, and startled easily. We had learned not to expect much from these short times together, but Mike was like a loaded spring, waiting to launch. His sleep at night was agitated. Again, I knew it was because he was only home for a short time.

Mike returned to Fallujah, Iraq, in time to do Christmas services. We celebrated without him at home. Of the previous three Christmases, Mike had only been home for one of them. Numbness continued to be my major feeling. I had failed to send goody boxes and letters. I had failed to bake cookies and cakes to mail to Mike. I had been so tired and numb this deployment that I had not emailed very often. I relied on the phone calls as our major way to communicate. I felt like a failure as a Navy wife, but the kids were continuing in a good lifestyle and our home was taken care of.

I knew when Mike returned that he would fill in the gaps that I was feeling. My expectations for his return were that he would be able to help me and I would not be so tired all of the time. Mike would see what needed to be done and help out. My best friend would be home so I could confide in someone. When Mike came home, I would be able to lean on him again and thus, be able to manage my life with RA.

Little did I know that halfway across the world, Mike was waiting to come home so that I could help him sort out the scenes that were playing and replaying in his head. He would be able to lean on me, his best friend, and life would make sense again. He could confide in me and I would ease his pain.

As Mike's third war experience ended, we both expected the other to relieve the pain and numbness that we had buried deep inside. We looked to each other to reignite the feelings that we both had numbed. Mike limped home, wounded deeply in spirit. I limped to pick him up, numbed in spirit and broken in body. These expectations are never the ones to have when reengaging after deployments of any kind, but especially not after war.

Our expectations of the other were never fulfilled as we found the effects of the war had moved home with Mike. Nothing prepared us for what was to come. Our need to be protected at home—Mike included—would deepen over the next few years.

CHAPTER THREE

"O Hear Us When We Cry to Thee"

How does a Navy Captain (06) ask for help for Post Traumatic Stress Disorder? How does a former Marine who taught hand-to-hand combat skills to Marine officers, who wears Expert rifle and pistol awards, and who was serving with the Marines in Iraq admit he suffers from PTSD? How does a chaplain who taught countless numbers of PTSD workshops and who has counseled hundreds of PTSD wounded admit he has PTSD? How does he admit he has PTSD when he is being offered the only Commanding Officer job in the entire Navy Chaplain Corps—and he is the first person selected for that position? How can he possibly show weakness when he needs to show strength through rank, through experience, and through position?

The answer to all of the above is: He doesn't. Mike did not ask for help and did not admit he was wounded. He didn't think he needed help. Time at home and a new job would take care of all of this. As he completed the psychological assessment when returning from Afghanistan and Iraq, he selectively answered the questions. He had used those forms as a chaplain so he knew all of the "right" answers. He didn't think what was raging in his mind and his dreams was a wound. He believed that home would provide the peace he sought. It always had before. He had successfully transitioned from deployment and a previous war, leaving the up-tempo pace behind. He didn't tell anyone about the chaos in his mind because he was afraid of many unknowns, including losing his Commanding Officer position. In retrospect, what he feared most was what was lurking inside his wound that had traumatized his spirit. As with most Marines and former Marines with PTSD, he bore the shame of having been to war and come home broken in spirit.

Times of Stress and Danger

In his powerful book, *Once a Warrior, Always a Warrior*, Charles Hoge (2010) describes military members' states of being when they return from the combat zone. He comments:

> Sometimes after coming home, warriors lose their ability to concentrate or focus when their body sets off alarm signals, like a pounding heart. In combat, you know exactly what to do when your anxiety ramps up. Back home, when anxiety warning bells go off it can be more difficult because you don't have a series of combat tasks or procedures to fall back on. (p. 94)

Hoge continues with descriptions of how warriors continually monitor their environment for threats in the combat zone. When the warriors return home, however, they often do not monitor their "internal perceptions of threat" and the behaviors that accompany those perceptions (Hoge, 2010, p. 94). When preparing for war or for deployment, military units and ships' crews begin to move into an "up-tempo" pace that continues throughout their deployment. This up-tempo pace includes work days that last eighteen hours, advanced training, advanced certifications to meet mission requirements, higher stress, a series of training packages tailored to specific military missions, heightened alertness as well as other training and drills that are meant to fine-tune the actions of the unit and the ship. During up-tempo times, the expectations are high and the stress is intensified.

The up-tempo pace that is within the combat zone takes on a heightened sense of purpose. Lives depend on split second decisions and on split second reactions. Over and over the military drills reactions into the men and women so that when they are under attack, they will respond according to their training. For our purposes in this book, we will use the term "up-tempo" to describe the intensified combat experiences that become the way of life to those serving in the combat zones.

In discussing problems that warriors experience in and after leaving the combat zone, Hoge notes the following:

> During times of stress and danger, the body is revved up due to adrenaline and other chemicals; the heart rate is increased, breathing becomes more rapid and shallow, muscle tension increases, and the mind becomes hyperalert. As a result, warriors are able to maintain high situational awareness, which is a very useful skill. This includes scanning the environment for anything that might be a threat, using their own fear or anxiety as a warning signal, and ensuring that they are always escape routes. (2010, p. 58)

Thus, warriors returning from the combat zone bring these necessary skills home with them. While these invaluable skills kept them alive in the combat zone, they find—as do their families—that these skills are not as valued when they return home.

Hoge presents the kinds of situations that can cause warriors to respond immediately with their high alert combat skills. These situations include:

> [A] crowd, a line of people, trash on the side of the road, overpasses, a hot day, someone asking "How are you?", sand, diesel fuel, traffic, a person of Middle Eastern or Vietnamese ethnicity, a loud noise, smoke, a movie image, a calendar date, a conversation about the war,

a helicopter overhead, someone not following through with something they were supposed to do, being boxed in somewhere, busy intersections, certain smells, etc. (2010, p. 135)

Hoge's list includes many common occurrences in our everyday life in the United States. Continuing, Hoge adds, "Numerous things can trigger reactions of anxiety, fear, and anger, or result in the warrior suddenly being flooded with images and feelings, bringing the war zone home or the warrior back to the war zone" (2010, p. 135). Often the family is unaware that an event, smell, sound, etc., has triggered the memories and they are bewildered by the actions of the warriors.

Because of the many changes that have occurred with warriors as a result of combat experience, the family tends to express confusion and dismay. Warriors tend to withdraw from events and social occasions because of the fear of triggering a reaction. "They retreat as far behind the front as they possibly can, and find the most secure bunker available" (Hoge, 2010, p. 135). This withdrawal leads to more confusion for the family and the warrior's return home becomes more difficult. "This tendency to avoid things can result in numerous problems because it conflicts with the expectations and desires of loved ones, friends, or coworkers for the warrior to do 'normal' things that people do" (Hoge, 2010, p. 135). When warriors return from the combat zone, they have had experiences that they need time to process. Avoiding activities and spending time "droning" allows warriors to process their experiences. These behaviors confuse families who have waited expectantly for their return.

Times of Confusion and Dismay

One June afternoon soon after Mike returned from Afghanistan, he decided it was time to clean the garage. Rounding up our three kids, Mike led them to the garage and assigned tasks to them. The boys, ages twelve and nineteen, were moving the items around while our daughter, age nine, swept around and under the items. Some boxes were earmarked for the trash so the boys were also to load those into Mike's truck.

After a few minutes, one of the kids ran inside to get another broom, leaving the garage door open. I heard Mike using a tone and voice he had never used with the kids. The essence was that our daughter didn't hold a broom correctly and the boys almost scratched the truck with a box. Our younger son had also almost dropped a box that wasn't trash.

I immediately went to the garage to see what was happening. Our daughter was in tears while she moved the broom around. Our sons were angry but not expressing it. Mike was standing there, red in the face and so angry.

I asked what was going on and he told me to go inside. When our first son was born, we had negotiated how we would discipline our children and what level of anger we would show them. Mike was outside the realm of any understanding that we had made in our marriage. From both of our childhoods, we had agreed that we would NEVER treat our children certain ways. Mike was ignoring all of our commitments and what for? A garage cleaning.

As Mike started telling the boys to get moving, I stepped in front of him to get his attention. "Why are you so angry? What happened?" I asked.

Mike, who is eleven inches taller than me, looked down at me and snarled, "I'm not angry. Leave me alone and go inside."

"No. What have the kids done?"

"GO INSIDE," Mike hurled at me. "I'm not angry. They just need to learn to work."

Mike had never spoken to me like that, especially in front of the kids. We never did that to each other. I was confused and the kids were bewildered. They continued to work rapidly in silence. Our daughter's tears kept falling. The tension, thick in the air, had silenced the kids. There was no laughter or teasing with this cleaning.

"Here, let me sweep," I suggested.

Mike turned to me and told me again to go inside. Furious at him, I went back inside. He finally took the broom from our daughter and finished the sweeping. The boys moved the boxes and then all three kids drove in the truck to the dumpster.

Mike refused to talk with me about the incident. He told me nothing had happened and that I needed to quit taking the kids' side. He also told me that he wasn't angry. The kids needed to learn to work. I argued with him about their ability to work and he finally walked into the bathroom, locked the door, and took a shower.

II Marine Expeditionary Force Forward Chaplain

While Mike was in Afghanistan during the Spring of 2006, Admiral Robert Burt was finishing his tour as the Chaplain of the Marine Corps. Fallujah and the Al Anbar province of Iraq were dangerous places as insurgents poured over the border from Jordan. Part of I MEF (Marine Expeditionary Force) from Camp Pendleton, CA, was in the Al Anbar Province of Iraq at that time and part of II MEF was preparing to go the following year.

When Mike returned from Afghanistan in May 2006, he was assigned to Camp Lejuene, NC, to be the Division Chaplain for 2D Marine Division. At the time, Admiral Burt was attempting to find a chaplain to be the II MEF FWD Chaplain—the chaplain with the II Marine Expeditionary Force Forward—but a number of senior chaplains refused the position. RADM Burt contacted Mike in late May 2006 to tell Mike that he would report to II MEF Forward to begin preparing for Iraq with the 2D Marine Division.

Admiral Burt, who would become the Chief of Chaplains in June 2006, told Mike that he did not have anyone else he could count on to do the job that needed to be done in Iraq. He acknowledged that Mike had only been home from a deployment for two weeks, but Admiral Burt stressed that Mike was the man best suited for the job at that time. Mike became part of II Marine Division and deployed with them six months after returning from Afghanistan.

Mike and I have recently discussed this conversation he had with Chaplain Burt. Knowing what this sort of turnaround from one war assignment to another would most likely do to Mike, Admiral Burt still reached out to Mike and assigned him that duty. Mike and I have discussed how difficult it must have been for him to do that, but Chaplain Burt had a bigger picture in mind. If we somehow could turn back time and be at that place again, Mike says that he would deploy again to Iraq, even though we know the price he paid. I also would encourage him to go, even though the cost was high. If it was not for Admiral Burt, we would not have come to be who we are today and we would not know what we know today about the grace of God and the hope that exists for those wounded in spirit.

As a result of this abnormally high deployment schedule, Admiral Burt appointed Mike to the position of Commanding Officer of the Naval Chaplaincy School when Mike returned from Iraq in February 2008. Mike would move to Newport, RI, in June 2008. Then he would move the Chaplains School to Columbia, SC, in the summer of 2009.

Arriving home in February, Mike found himself with little to no time to readjust to life in our family and in the United States. In the four months between when Mike arrived home from Iraq and we moved to Newport, RI, Mike had to complete the following:

- Plan a Memorial Service for all of the Marines who died during the time II MEF was deployed in Iraq. The families of 112 Marines traveled from all over the United States. Mike planned and conducted the service for these Marines. When he was in Iraq, Mike had attended the Memorial Services that were held in country for each of the 112 Marines, sailors, and soldiers as well as the other people who were killed in action (KIA) that year.

- Attend Command Leadership School in Newport, Rhode Island, in order to learn to become a CO. The information that he learned in that course was necessary as he took command of the Naval Chaplains School. This school lasted four weeks.

- Attend the Legal Course for Commanding Officers for two weeks.

- Prepare his office and his home for a move. Because he was not deployed, Mike had to complete the paperwork involved with the move.

- Readjust to family life after two successive year-long combat deployments.

It was easier to place his feelings on the back burner, letting them simmer there.

PTSD Never Just Simmers

Mike and I attended a school for prospective Commanding Officers and their spouses in April of that time period. This week away gave Mike and me time to be together. We had looked forward to it and we enjoyed our time together. We talked some but we both were still so tired and numb. The damp, cold wind in Newport stiffened my joints so that I had difficulty moving. I tried to keep up with Mike's long strides, but the stiffness won out and Mike received his first lesson in the physical changes that had happened to me in his absence. I feared that he would be upset that I had changed so much. I hoped that with a bit of time, all would begin to flow well for us since we were such "old hands" with deployments.

Mike's school lasted several weeks while mine lasted a week. Upon his return home, Mike formalized the plans for the memorial services that II MEF was holding for the men and women who died in Iraq. I took off work, planning to accompany Mike to the service.

Two days before the service, I asked Mike to confirm the times and to tell me the location. "It's at Camp Lejeune," Mike said.

When Mike understood that I was going, he said, "You don't need to go. There's no point I'll be really busy with the families." He then told me how many families were coming and from how far away.

"I've taken off work and I was going to come to support you," I responded, bewildered at his words. I had always gone to these kinds of services as a support for Mike at the very least. Mike had always wanted me to go.

"You don't need to come. I'll be really busy," he responded.

"Are you sure? I was planning to come."

"No point. Just stay here. You don't need to miss work," he responded very matter-of-factly as he opened a book to begin to read.

That was my first real exposure to the change that had come over my husband. I left the room quietly and went for a walk to cry. He had been gone for so long and he no longer wanted me to support him. How had that happened? What was going on? I had no idea but I knew deep inside that something was very wrong. This incident hurt me deeply. I wasn't sure what had changed between us, but when Mike insisted that I stay home, he hurt me deeply.

Mike, however, has told me that he had no idea that he hurt me. He was, instead, sparing me from having to remember the deaths, the bodies, the trauma of the combat zone. The fact that those were *his* feelings that he assumed I would also feel is irrational to him now. He can't explain what he was feeling and thinking, but he insists that he was thinking first of protecting me. This incident is an excellent example of how the thought processes of warriors returning from the combat zone are not always working in the logical arena. (Mike's prayer that he prayed at the memorial service is Appendix A and his sermon that he delivered at that memorial service is Appendix B.)

We prepared for the move and I found that I was unable to complete the tasks that I had so easily done in the past. Separating items for giving away or throwing away became overwhelming. I had always preferred to move in with a lighter load, but our move to Newport became one that moved items we no longer wanted. The move felt heavy and cluttered.

Commanding Officer: Naval Chaplaincy School and Center

We arrived for our second Newport, Rhode Island, tour in June 2008. Knowing we would only be there a year, we wanted to take advantage of the summer time in New England. We also had Mike's Change of Command ceremony to plan. Our time was full and we moved in as rapidly as possible since we would soon have family and friends attending the Change of Command.

When all of the summer activities passed, Mike began a schedule of flying out for several days and then flying back for the weekends as the plans for moving the Chaplains School to Columbia, SC, were formed. The buildings were being built and every detail had to be overseen. We mainly saw each other on the weekends.

When Mike was home, I began to notice many changes with him. At nights, Mike would yell out in his sleep. He would fight the covers with his legs pumping and his fists grabbing at the covers. I would try to wake him, but he would just say something incomprehensible to me, settle down for a few minutes, and then begin his thrashing and crying out again. Some nights, Mike would throw off the covers and wake me to say, "Go turn down the heat!" as the wind blew frigid air through the cracks and crevices in the windows. No night brought restful sleep for him.

Shoes and boots...who would think that shoes and boots could create such havoc? Our house in Newport was built around 1875 and had had sections added to it during renovations. The entry from the driveway was one of the changed areas of the house. The door opened into an L-shaped short hall that contained the washer and dryer and opened immediately into the kitchen. Clothes were often stacked in the hall to go into the washer or folded on the dryer waiting to go upstairs to the bedrooms. From our previous experience in Newport, I knew what kind of muck and mess shoes and boots left in the house from the sand, ice, and snow, so I required the kids to remove their shoes and boots at the doorway. It seemed the practical solution to keeping the house clean.

One day, Mike came in the door and I saw boots and shoes flying into the kitchen. Some of them landed on the dirty clothes in the basket. I left supper preparations to see what was happening.

Mike pushed past me and yelled upstairs for each of the kids. They came running down. He then told them to keep the boots and shoes out of the doorway and to take them to their rooms.

I immediately protested because I didn't want the dirt and mess all over the house.

Mike insisted on the footwear going to the rooms.

I suggested that he might want to clean the mess that the boots left. We then escalated the argument from there that also included the clothes that were in the hallway in front of the washer on wash days. I said that I had no other choice because I physically was unable to walk up and down the stairs with the clothes. I also pointed out that they were only there on wash days. Mike yielded on the clothes but was adamant on the boots and shoes. In this encounter, I went back to my theme of the last year—"Why are you so angry?" Mike continually denied that he was angry, but I had no other interpretation for his approach. Mike finally left the kitchen and said to eat without him

The kids came down the back staircase. I told them to start leaving their shoes and boots at the side porch door. They asked why their dad was so mad. I really had no answer for them. They also pointed out that there was no heat at the side porch door and their boots would freeze. I told them that I would talk with their dad later. Mike wouldn't discuss it. He was adamant that the kids needed to learn to clean up which meant placing shoes and boots in their rooms. I didn't understand why this was so important to him. I also didn't understand why my solution wasn't acceptable. We ended up with dribble messes all the way to the kids' rooms.

I began to see more and more that Mike was having difficulty fitting in with our family life. He had been home long enough to adjust, but we were drifting further apart. This kind of rift had never been part of our marriage. We were a seasoned Navy couple who had grown stronger and closer through deployments and through our first war experience. I knew, however, that something was wrong. I went online to read about Post Traumatic Stress Disorder and several other possibilities. I had vaguely known what PTSD was and I knew that Mike knew from his work.

I read about the symptoms of PTSD (see Appendix C) and I knew that Mike was exhibiting many of them. Mike admits that he also knew he was exhibiting them, but he did not know how to help himself. I knew that I had to find a way to reach Mike. I collected my terms, planned my approach, and began a conversation with Mike about PTSD. The conversation did not go well. In retrospect, I presented my information analytically which Mike interpreted as an attack. He then responded as though I were attacking him; however, I was not going to give up.

A few days later, I sent Mike an email, thinking that I could write the information better than I could discuss it. It was a long involved e-mail that, in retrospect, was highly argumentative. The email served to accuse more than motivate. I had again failed to communicate with my husband. What I didn't understand at the time was that Mike's primary motivation was self-protection—a necessary skill in combat zones. We had always had excellent communication between us. But with the failure of the email, I felt that our communication had broken down completely.

I began to pray that God would help Mike to understand what I was trying to say. I asked God to help me understand what was going on with Mike. I asked God to heal Mike. I asked Him to help me communicate with Mike. I cried out often to God and, after enough time, wasn't sure I was heard.

I would then stand up from those prayers and begin to communicate with Mike as I always had. I did not give God a chance to teach me, but, instead, continued to use the communication skills that had always been successful for me in the past. I failed in my attempts to bridge the gap that existed between Mike and me.

I also began passive-aggressive behaviors that I knew would irritate Mike, but I couldn't think of any other way to avoid the anger. Somehow, after so many years of marriage, I could no longer match and fold his clothes exactly right. I would agree with some of his analysis since my poorly controlled rheumatoid arthritis made my hands swollen and stiff. I could fold his T-shirts well enough, but definitely not up to Marine standards. I had a very difficult time matching the socks and then rolling them correctly. After enough encounters over socks—socks!!—I just said I was unable to fold them. I stopped matching them, used my disease as an excuse, and felt guilty for opting out in such a passive-aggressive way. That, however, gave me a bit of relief from what I interpreted as Mike's anger over such small, insignificant things.

I began to realize that I could not help Mike. At this point, we had a complete breakdown of the communication that had flowed so easily between us before he went to war. The words from my mouth became angrier and I found myself challenging Mike often. I found that I did not trust Mike as my best friend anymore. Losing Mike's friendship was the most painful part of this time. Our marriage was unrecognizable; yet, I did not see leaving Mike as an option.

Mike's wound had come from his time at war. I had committed to him through our marriage vows, but I also had committed to support our family at home so that he could support the service members fighting for our country. I could not walk away from such responsibility. My husband came home wounded from war...what sort of person would I be if I just left him? So I responded to duty with a less than caring attitude. I also committed to somehow getting Mike help.

I went to a close friend of ours who was also working at the Chaplains School. This friend had been stationed in Iceland when we had been there. He had come to dinner every Tuesday evening for his two-year tour in Iceland, carving a place in our family with those visits. Mike and I both trusted our friend completely. I confided in him what was happening with Mike and me. Our friend listened but did not tell me what he would do.

Approaching Mike in his office, our friend suggested that Mike find help, giving him the name of the Naval Medical Clinic psychiatrist that I had provided to our friend. Unable to listen to me and unable to help himself, Mike listened to this trusted friend and began to meet with the base psychiatrist. Mike continued with her for the remainder of our tour.

I was relieved that Mike decided to talk with the psychiatrist. I relaxed, feeling confident that Mike would begin to sleep deeply and would find relief from his PTSD. I thought that a few sessions and all would be well again. I was naive.

Mike's first experience in counseling symbolized, for him, that he needed to change in some way. He admitted that he needed to adjust and to change his reactions, understandings, and meanings. The actuality of the change, however, took time to be processed. It was not a rapid change, but instead, was a slow adjustment that happened incrementally over time.

When war traumatizes the spirit, a person needs time to heal. Time comes in years and not in a few sessions. The reading I had done on the Internet did more harm than good to our marriage and our friendship. I now understand that time and many other elements are necessary for a service member's spirit to begin to heal from their war wounds.

Respite from the War: A Beginning

At this time, my prayers continued to be closer to demands for God to help me understand what was happening. My prayer and Mike's separate prayers took the form of cries for help more than any other kind of prayer. I played a certain song over and over so that I could hear the line that contained the words, "a respite from the war." That became my prayer. I asked over and over for a respite from the war. I am not sure that my prayers took any other form than a continual pleading for a respite from the war for my husband and my family.

After we moved to Columbia, SC, in the summer of 2009, Mike continued to have PTSD symptoms. He retired from active duty in the summer of 2011. It was the next summer that Mike said he wanted to go back to counseling. During Mike's second counseling experience, my heart changed and I learned the depth of the wound that my husband suffered.

Mike bought a book recommended by his counselor. The book, *Once a Warrior, Always a Warrior,* by Charles W. Hoge, MD, a retired Army Colonel, is the best resource that Mike brought home from this therapy experience. Mike experienced a great deal of outward growth from this time in counseling. I experienced a tremendous shift in my approach to PTSD as I began to read the book.

I thought I understood PTSD from websites and articles that I had read. Until I read this book, I was blind, acting from poor understandings of the symptoms. I was overwhelmed that my husband had been having so many fears and struggles. I had had no idea that he was so far from me. The worst part, however, was that I had unknowingly exacerbated his symptoms by assuming that we were both still the same as we had been before the war and then relating to Mike from that stance.

Because of the significance of this book in our lives, we will use Hogue's book to communicate what Mike was thinking and/or responding to and, in contrast, explain what I had thought his motivations were through the language provided by Dr. Hoge. To this point, we have related my interpretations of events and my analysis of Mike's motivations. In Chapter 4 "For Those in Peril on the Sea," we will begin introducing Mike's motivations and his interpretations of events. The chapter will begin, however, with Mike's war experiences and continue through his return to a world that no longer made sense and a family that did not understand his changes. We will begin to relate how God *did* hear us when we cried to Him.

CHAPTER FOUR

"For Those in Peril on the Sea"

For a few years, Kathy told me that part of the reason that I came home with PTSD is that I had spent so much time at war. I argued for a while but when I really was able to think about it, she was right. I had spent three years either in a combat zone, preparing for combat, or dealing with the aftermath. The up-tempo pace had become my lifestyle. It seemed like a shallow excuse for not being able to do my duty and then readjust when I got home.

Kathy tried to get me to talk to her, but I never could find the words. I knew that it hurt her because I had always talked to her about what was bothering me. I knew that she wouldn't understand—not really. I couldn't understand all of what had happened so how could she? I would just walk away and close up. I couldn't even explain why I couldn't talk to her. I just couldn't.

In Newport, I had so many responsibilities as the Commanding Officer. I had to oversee the staff, the schoolhouse, the moving of the school to Columbia SC, the moving of the Religious Program Specialist (RP) School from Meridian MS to Columbia, the building of the new chaplain school facilities in Columbia, and on and on. I was on the road every other week. When I was home, I just wanted quiet. I didn't want to think. I didn't want to talk. I didn't want to feel. I wanted to escape from all that was going on inside of me. I just wanted to be in a cocoon where I could feel safe. I just wanted numbness.

With three kids in the house, however, there was no way to have that quiet that I longed for. I wanted quiet and I wanted peace, but I couldn't find it at home. Kathy was still trying to talk with me. I finally just barked at her and she dropped the idea of counseling. Or I thought she had.

Counseling: First Round

I did not know until a few years later that Kathy had prompted our close friend from Iceland to talk with me. I must admit that Kathy picked the perfect person to present the idea of going to counseling. I am not sure I would have allowed anyone else to talk to me like that, but this friend and I had a deep friendship that went back to Iceland. He even had the name and phone number of the base psychiatrist who specialized in PTSD…which, years later, I found out Kathy had supplied to him.

At this time, the question that kept going through my head was "Where does a chaplain go when he needs a chaplain?" I decided that maybe this was the place to go. It was almost by accident that I finally set up the appointment. I was at the Navy medical clinic in Newport taking care of another issue. I walked by the psychiatrist's office. I stopped and re-read the sign for the psychiatrist's office. My mind was racing. I was hurting so much and knew that I needed to go into the office. I wanted to stop the numbness, pain, nightmares, and overwhelming stress. I'm not sure why I stopped at the door, but I distinctly remember an urgency, a sort of restlessness that caused me to enter the office. Now, I recognize that the Holy Spirit prompted me to go into the office; but at the time, I just wanted relief from the chaos in my spirit. I entered the office and set up an appointment. I had to complete the mental health assessments again. This time, I completed all parts of the assessment with accurate answers. I cannot explain how torn I was with going to that first appointment.

I knew going would be a mistake because I was a Commanding Officer and a Navy Captain. After all, chaplains and CO's aren't supposed to have these problems. While I knew that was a false assumption—I had even taken issue with the assumption when talking with others—it was what I felt at the time. The risk of seeking help could end my time as CO and cause me great humiliation. I could be removed from my command if the Admiral learned that I was having problems and was so broken inside. I would have nowhere else to go after such humiliation. Seeking help could end my career. I loved the Navy chaplaincy and did not want my career to end that way.

I knew going would be a mistake because I was a chaplain and had counseled hundreds of men and women with PTSD. I knew how it worked. I knew what to say. I knew all about it. I also knew that I was struggling with PTSD and it was affecting many aspects of my life that I treasured. Sometimes I even thought I could heal myself with my knowledge.

I knew going would be a mistake because I was a Marine and good Marines do not struggle with these issues. I felt that I had failed to live up to the code that Marines have because I went to war and came home with PTSD.

I knew going would be a mistake because I was a minister and I taught how God could be with us through all circumstances. I believed that with my whole heart and being. My Christian faith seemed not to be helping me. Prayers struggled to find their way out of my spirit when so much chaos was running free through my spirit, mind, and body.

I knew going would be a mistake because I was in my fifties and I knew all about war, about PTSD, and about myself. I was not a young man who was shocked by what he encountered. I had seen and experienced so many traumatic events. I had walked with so many people as they made their way through the ruins of that trauma. I was experienced and I should be able to understand what was going on with me. I should be able to handle it.

I also knew the professional language and the theories of combat stress and PTSD. I had studied this material in courses and in workshops. I had taught workshops and counseled many people. Yet, none of that protected me. I was being eaten alive by the stress and chaos in my spirit. I just kept denying it and pushing it deeper inside of me.

But I went to counseling. I went in hopes of calming the chaos that raged through my spirit. I went in hopes of being able to sleep through the night. I went because I had no other choice. I went because I had nowhere else to go.

So much of what I had believed—the way the world made sense to me—had been turned upside down. I did not realize it at the time but I was stuck in an up-tempo pace for life. Living for three years in an up-tempo pace had reset me to that pace. I do not remember a lot of details from our family life in Newport. I just remember that no one would respond fast enough and they didn't care enough about the details. Intense focus on details is what keeps you alive in the combat zone and the details can't be ignored. Looking back, I understand that my family was not aware of the dangers that existed. I was aware of those dangers and, as the man of the house, I had to protect my family. At the time, I had not distinguished that the dangers in the combat zone were not the dangers at home. It didn't occur to me to make that distinction. I was trying to protect my family from what I now knew was out there. They didn't ever respond quickly enough and they never were serious enough about the dangers and threats.

Kathy irritated me a good bit. While I understood that she had rheumatoid arthritis and that it was debilitating, I did not really understand it because I had not slowed down enough to actually grasp the differences in her. Kathy had always taken care of the family, the house, the meals, the kids, and me. My up-tempo pace collided with her slow, stiff pace. She moved so slowly and she put us in so much danger. Then she would argue with me when I tried to explain it to her. It seems strange now, but that was what I felt at the time: "She's got to move faster!"

I had so hoped that coming home would take care of what was destroying my spirit. Kathy was supposed to help me and I longed to have her fix me or at least help me fix it. I know now that my expectations were misplaced. As a chaplain, I have told hundreds of couples that they cannot fix each other. Yet, my spirit longed for peace. As my closest friend, I wanted her to help me. She has told me that she had the same expectations of me, but in my up-tempo pace, I never even noticed.

Robert Grant (1996) states:

> To be cast out of social connectedness and to become marginalised is quite frightening. At the same time it is usually only the marginalised who recognise the social madness and denial that passes for "normality."... Victims of trauma are often the only ones who recognise which social structures are keeping its citizens in the dark. (p. 34)

The concept of marginalization was part of my reluctance to seek help. I didn't want to be pushed to the side. After experiencing trauma, however, people begin to feel marginalized by the "normal" members of society.

Grant continues by explaining that trauma victims feel cast out of their normal lives which often are lives that are an illusion of reality. In other words, people build lives based on the myths of our culture: We can always look young, we will never die, BFFs (best friends forever) are always trustworthy, etc. Thus, when trauma occurs, these myths rupture and trauma victims realize that their former reality was only an illusion. Only by embracing the spiritual path can the traumatized find growth.

> The path of the marginalised involves uncertainty, shame, and danger. Finding the way back to people... is not an easy task. The path of the marginalised is the path of all trauma victims. It is also the path of liberation

and spiritual growth. To be marginal is to be cast out of the "taken for granted" which in many cases is a blind, sedated and thus illusionary version of reality. (Grant, 1996, p. 34)

I was not, however, in a position to embrace a spiritual journey toward healing. I needed to stabilize more before I could begin this journey. I wanted a quick fix so that the night sweats, the nightmares, and the images of death and brokenness that filled my mind would go away—fast. I did find several less than helpful approaches, including the "old/new normal" explanation.

Many of the explanations of PTSD would say that I had a "new normal" and we needed to learn to embrace that new normal. This explanation follows this line of reasoning:

- I left our "normal" life when I began preparations to leave for Afghanistan (all two weeks of preparation).

- When I arrived in Afghanistan, I learned a "new normal" which I lived in for the next three years. I view the memorial service at Camp Lejeune as the ending of my combat experiences.

- I brought the "new normal" home and that did not match with the "normal" of our family.

- This line of thought then proposes that I need to learn to be "normal" again. Or I need to find something called a "new normal."

Kathy and I reject this concept of having a "new normal." There is nothing normal about the up-tempo, intensely focused lifestyle I led in the combat zones. The up-tempo pace is what kept me alive in Afghanistan and Iraq. The up-tempo pace is not something to throw away in hopes of a normal life. There are positives to the up-tempo pace so disposing of those skills means warriors may not be ready to return to combat.

There is nothing normal about living in a constant state of high situational awareness. Every item, every movement, every word could be a warning of a coming attack. There is nothing normal about living in a protective shell that protects me from the ones who love me most. These up-tempo lifestyle changes should never be classified as "normal" even though they are the norm for combat zones. They are abnormal in almost every way possible. Using "new normal" is a marginalization of the trauma to the spirit, mind, and body that warriors experience in the combat zone.

Kathy and I have discussed this concept of a "new normal." It is counterintuitive to the concept of reconnecting after deployments—war or otherwise. The post-deployment readjustment requires an acknowledgement that each family member has grown and changed during the deployment cycle. Readjustment does not require remembering the "normal" life that existed before deployment, but readjustment requires the deployed family member learning the new family patterns and adjusting to the new flow of family life. The family adjusts to the changes in the service member and the natural flow of life continues. Including the word, "normal," means that there is a "normal" (which is questionable to begin with) and that normal is the goal of healing. We will argue that normal is not the goal; instead, posttraumatic growth through spiritual change is the goal.

Additionally, how can we go to war, see what we have seen, smell what we have smelled, participate in what we have participated in, experience what we have experienced, and then return to a "normal" life? War is a traumatic experience that changes each person who is part of the terror and horror of the experience. During the time in the combat zone, war is hell. During so many days after we return, war is still hell. Hell is a very dark reality. "Normal" should not be a goal of those returning from war. The world as we knew it before the war no longer exists. Our war experience no longer fits the patterns and the concepts that we had of life, of people, and of God.

Mary Beth Werdel and Robert J. Wicks (2012), in *Primer on Posttraumatic Growth,* discuss this change that trauma brings. Most people—especially in the Western world—have a set of beliefs that are as follows: "The world is safe; bad things do not happen to good people; young people are not supposed to die" (p. xi). Traumatic events like those that occur in combat zones "shatter these basic assumptions, resulting in experiences of distress as well as a sense of loss of control, meaning, and predictability" (Werdel & Wicks, 2012, p. xi). Combat exposure challenges the basic beliefs of the people involved.

Grant continues this line of thought when he comments:

> Trauma exposes the insubstantiality of what victims cherish the most. It unmistakably shows victims that they are limited creatures whose desires can only be realised in something other than status, material possessions and co-dependent relationships. Humans are transcendentally needy. Ultimate meaning can only be found when victims acknowledge their fundamental inability to ensure self-sufficiency and safety. This acknowledgement facilitates more comprehensive ways of relating to life's most profound dimensions. (1996, p. 35)

I knew that I had been traumatized, but I wanted to ignore it. I wanted to be free from all of this. I wanted the world the way it had been…only I knew that world would never come back. I could no longer "maintain the status quo" even though I resisted "opening up reality until [I] absolutely had to" (Grant, 1996, p. 37).

As I thought about counseling, I felt overwhelmed. How could I find a way to verbalize all of the events, thoughts, feelings, smells, dreams? Grant describes "trauma" in the following definition:

> Trauma is not just an event but a constellation of meanings and relationships. Side effects, fears, betrayals, losses of innocence, failures to be understood and the reorganisation of beliefs are all part of the trauma constellation. Trauma demands a change of visions…It activates a profound questioning that differentiates humans from all other forms of life. Trauma is an invitation to change and to pass through the deepest centre of one's nature and come out on the other side. (1996, p. 38)

I wasn't sure that I could face the trauma. I wasn't sure that I had the time to commit to counseling. My major question at this time was "Where is God in all of this?" I did not want to feel so isolated and alone. I was, after all, a chaplain—a bearer of the presence of God. How could I be so wounded?

During our year in Newport, I traveled extensively. I went to Columbia SC, Pensacola FL, Norfolk VA, Meridian MS, Washington DC, and several other places. I did, however, keep my first appointment with the psychiatrist. Much to my surprise, I found someone who I could talk to. This psychiatrist was a retired Navy Captain. Thus, many of the pressures of my job were ones she could understand. I truly grew to trust her. There was no condemnation, no judgments, and no indication that I was a failure or a poor Christian.

I realized with all of my reasons for avoiding counseling that my spirit could no longer contain the chaos churning inside me. Seeking counseling was one of the hardest admissions I had ever made to myself. I needed help and it was not Kathy or my job or anything else. I needed help to create order from the disorder that the up-tempo pace and the listening to story after story after story from warriors had brought to my spirit. There were times when my dreams were their stories. The details were vivid as if I had been there myself. I dreamed the stories they told me, hearing the screams, smelling the smells, experiencing the horror, and seeing the death. Their stories became my nightly experiences.

I went to counseling the remainder of my tour in Newport. I was able to share stories and experiences that I could not seem to share with Kathy or with anyone. I told my stories and I found that, in telling the stories, they had less power over me. This first round of counseling was very helpful to me. Kathy, however, reports that she did not see a great change.

Chaplains are high on the list of PTSD sufferers. They have a type of PTSD called "secondary PTSD" which means that listening to the stories of the war fighters hour after hour, day after day, and week after week, affects their ability to process trauma. Listening to trauma over and over can traumatize the person who listens. Family members of military members with PTSD often suffer this secondary PTSD as well. The "basic world assumptions of direct victims of trauma are often upset, so too are the assumptions of indirect victims" (Dekel & Solomon, 2007, p. 149). When I was in Iraq, I didn't consider the possibilities of secondary PTSD. Instead, I did my job of listening to those attempting to make meaning from their experiences, helping where I could, and all of the other duties that were expected of me.

As the senior chaplain in the Al Anbar Province, I listened to my chaplains as they would come back from the outposts and need to share their stories. I listened to the senior officers as they unburdened some of their stories. I was in vehicles that were part of convoys hit by IEDs. I accompanied the General as he visited each outpost on Thanksgiving Day and then again on Christmas Day. I was in a helicopter that was almost shot down. That incident brought back the memory of standing in the combat operations center two weeks prior. We all watched in horror as a helicopter crashed and began burning. The burned bodies were pulled from the wreckage on multiple screens. These images, seared in my mind, played as the helicopter went silent.

I could continue but which of these things was the one thing that affected me? I did not have the answer to that. Grant (1996) develops the concept of "secondary traumatization" when he explains:

> Those who constantly bear witness to the wounds of others absorb trauma vicariously.... Internalising the pain of another can disrupt personal frames of meaning and lead to feelings of powerlessness. Continually seeing or hearing stories of pain and horror can challenge a professional's basic beliefs about self and society, as well as his/her need to be competent and in control. (p. 14)

I absorbed trauma from those around me. Their stories became my dreams. Their horrors became a part of me.

Patrick Meadors and Angela Lamson (2008) describe "compassion fatigue and secondary traumatization" as dependent on three criteria: "proximity, intensity, and duration." My wife's theory is that I was in an up-tempo life for so long with no down time that I was affected. She also thinks my initial training as a Marine Infantry Officer (with the expert pistol and rifle awards) exaggerated my feelings of helplessness when, as a chaplain, I had no weapon in the combat zones. Ultimately, I do not know why I came home from war with a diagnosis of severe PTSD. But my proximity, intensity, and duration did affect me.

I do know that the counseling helped me bring some order to my life, but there was so much that was still in disorder. Our move to Columbia, SC in September 2009 ended my counseling in Newport. I benefited from the counseling, but, as with most counseling, immediate changes do not happen. Time brings changes.

Graduation Day

One of the best examples of how Kathy and I were unknowingly living in different worlds is our oldest son's graduation from college that May before we moved from Newport. Michael had chosen to move back to Newport with us, completing the rest of his college with online courses offered by the university.

Campbell University sits in a very small town about an hour from Raleigh, NC. It is a tranquil and peaceful place. We arrived early, parked, and found seats in the new coliseum. My father had come to the graduation from Oklahoma. Kathy's father (who was moving deeper into dementia) and her sister came from South Carolina. There were seven of us sitting in the upper deck of the new coliseum.

When graduation was over, everyone in the coliseum began heading for the doors. My father disappeared and Kathy, her father, and sister were separated from us as we went through the doors to the stairs. Kathy insists on taking over the story at this part, but I will tell the true story after she tells her part.

Kathy: We were five people behind Mike and the kids. Dad and I were having trouble walking down the stairs so more people passed us. I had been sick all night with a stomach virus. I was very weak and stiff, but Dad and I finally made it to the bottom.

Mike was just outside of the door, waiting. I could tell that he was not happy with how slow we were, but what did it matter? Michael would be a few minutes anyway and then we would be taking pictures.

Mike told me to stand next to a tree and keep my dad, sister, and daughter with me. He took Jeff and went to find his father. We stood as people cleared out. Michael came wandering around the corner of the building and stood with us for a few minutes. Then he decided to find his father. Since we were just standing and I wanted to start pictures, I told Michael to bring all three of the missing family members back to us.

I tried again to call Mike, but we were so far out in the boonies that I did not have a signal. Michael came around the building, saying that he could not find his father or grandfather but he had found Jeff.

I was ready to leave because I felt so weak. "Let's go to the back of the building and see if we can find them." So we all meandered back to the back of the coliseum, admiring the flowers along the way.

Mike was not back there so I sent the boys around the other side of the building. They came back, following their father. "Where have you been? Why didn't you stay where I told you to?" Mike hissed in my ear.

I was confused. What had him so upset?

"We need to take pictures," I said.

"We can't. We have to go NOW," Mike replied. Mike hates pictures, especially when we have to pose with so many different groupings. Ordinarily, I would give in, but this was a graduation. It only happens once in a lifetime.

"We have to have pictures. We'll never get the chance again," I stated. Mike glared at me and I fought back tears.

"We'll get them at the hotel," Mike responded, more impatiently.

"I want them here," I said. It was graduation. Why would I want to take them at the hotel?

The five in our immediate family stood for three pictures before Mike said that we had to get in the cars. Mike found his dad who had gone to change from a suit to blue jeans, rounded us all into the car and sped out of the parking lot.

From our oldest son's college graduation, we have three pictures of the five of us. We have none of either grandfather or of his aunt. I was crushed, embarrassed, and angry.

Mike's story, however, paints a different picture.

Mike: When we stood up from the graduation, I noticed the large bags that the women were carrying. We had sat near the exit but if any of those bags exploded, I could not keep my family safe. Our best bet was to go down the stairs as quickly as possible and find safety outside of the building. We at least had options outside.

Kathy and her family poked their way down the stairs, oblivious to the dangers. Why does she always have to fight me on this?

I gave them a place to stand so that I could find my father and Michael and we could get out of there. So many people were pouring out of multiple doors. I tried to do a threat assessment but I was overwhelmed with the backpacks and the purses that people had. I had to protect my family. We needed to get out of there.

I had left Kathy and her family on the left side of the building but, after looking for my father, I forgot which side I had left them on. There were so many people. They stood around in groups with some of them looking around. I could not assess the threats. Were they looking at me? Where was my family? Didn't Kathy see this danger? Why wasn't she bringing her father to safety?

When I found them, I was so relieved. I needed to get them out of that whole area. They needed to be safe. Kathy insisted on pictures. Didn't she understand that standing still like that made us even bigger targets?

And where did my father go? How can I protect all of these people that I love when they are working against me?

I tried to tell Kathy, but she started that crying stuff. Why would she cry when I'm protecting them? What is wrong with her lately? There is danger everywhere.

Everyone finally got in their cars and we were able to leave that place. I drove like I had in Afghanistan. Kathy didn't understand how important leaving the scene as fast as possible and making yourself as small a target as possible was to our family's safety.

When we arrived back at the hotel, I felt I had done my duty. I had saved my family from the hidden dangers. I had protected them and they were safe. Why was everyone looking at me that way?

This story best exemplifies the two worlds in which Kathy and I lived. I lived in a state of constantly being in peril on the sea. We were unable to bridge that gap though I tried many ways once we moved to Columbia. In Chapter 5, I will explain trauma and the way I understood my actions and my life. We will move into how Kathy learned to understand the wound in Chapter 6. We still pray that God will shield our brothers and sisters in danger's hour.

CHAPTER FIVE

"Our Brethren Shield in Danger's Hour"

Stress is a common feature of daily life. How people handle stress results from a variety of incidents, experiences, and emotions. No one is sure why people who are exposed to the same stressors react differently—some experience extreme stress while others experience more moderate stress. Some of the reasons include family histories and previous experiences. War is a highly stressful experience that keeps warriors in the up-tempo pace for extended periods of time. War and the experience of the combat zone is in a category of stress unto itself. Examining stress and the ensuing reactions in the combat zone is essential for understanding warriors who return from the combat zone with a PTSD diagnosis.

In war, we woke up every day with an awareness of danger and of knowing that this could be our last day on earth. I lived in a compound in Kabul, Afghanistan, which routinely received random gunfire or an occasional missile. As I traveled to different commands around Kabul, I often was the driver of our vehicle because, under the Geneva Conventions, I was unarmed. I drove so that we had more weapons posed to defend us if necessary. My situational awareness was fine-tuned in Afghanistan because of the randomness of vehicle attacks or riots or IEDs. The constant need to be aware of every detail in the environment and every person who entered the area created an extremely high stress environment. I lived in an extreme up-tempo environment for eleven months. I responded to sounds before my mind registered them. I was purposeful in where my gear was stored at night and during the day so that if any alerts went off, I could respond without thinking. My driving became fine-tuned so that I drove at top speeds through town, staying on the bumper of the car in front of me. These are part of the up-tempo lifestyle that kept me, and those with me, alive. I lived in this intensity hourly as my six-month tour stretched to eleven months.

Many situations create daily stress in our daily lives in America, including traffic backups, arguments with family or friends, car problems, projects for work, and many other events that are called "stressors." Roni Berger(2015) defines a "stressor event" as "a life situation which places a demand or pressure on an individual, a family, or a community that produces, or has the potential to produce, a major change from the previous state so that regular responses cannot effectively address it" (p. 5). When our regular responses to events fail to adequately address some experiences, the result is stress. Some stress, however, is longer-term stress such as the loss of a job, struggling to pay bills, and similar occurrences. Berger describes these events as a "pile-up of stressors," which "refers to the build-up of multiple stressful situations, which occur simultaneously and may lead to stress becoming a chronic condition in the life of the individual, family, or community. Stress pile-up can occur as a result of a continuous problem in the social environment (such as the decades of war in Afghanistan)" (Berger, 2015, pp. 5-6). In the combat zone, stressors continually "pile-up" since existence in these zones produces a continual high stress environment.

Riots routinely occurred in Kabul, Afghanistan and if NATO personnel were caught in those riots, then they were brutally treated by the rioters. Leaving the compound always carried the threat of being caught up in riots. The military leadership attempted to work with the Afghan government to quell the riots and bring a semblance of peace to the city.

In October 2005, reports came to us of the desecration of Taliban bodies. Aghans flowed into Kabul and began staging massive riots that became larger and larger by the day. Special Forces soldiers had urinated on dead Taliban fighters, burned their bodies, and filmed the activities. The Muslim faith requires bodies to be buried within twenty-four hours of death. The desecration of these bodies by the Special Forces soldiers angered the country with massive rioting as the result.

In my role as the Theater Chaplain, I was sent to meet with the Afghan Minister of Hajj and Islamic Affairs, Nematullah Shahrani. As an Afghan Cabinet member, Minister Shahrani had written the Sharia Law section of the Afghanistan constitution. As we talked, I assured him that the soldiers responsible for the desecration were being held responsible. After listening to my message, Minister Shahrani agreed to calm the riots. He was meeting with 300 mullahs that evening at 1900 and would tell them to stop the rioting.

The problem was that it was 1500 when I left his office—four hours before he would meet with the mullahs. As our three-vehicle convoy wove through the streets of Kabul, we entered a large, open area where three major roads met. As our humvees squealed to a stop, everyone in the convoy began cursing. The area was full of Afghans looking to riot. They spotted us and began closing in around us. Several rocks were thrown our way. Fists were shaking at us and people were screaming at us. The third vehicle didn't back up because the orders were to follow the first vehicle. We couldn't back up and we couldn't go forward. There were hundreds of Afghans armed with rocks, sticks, and more dangerous weapons beginning to move our way.

As the mass moved closer to us, someone spotted a small street off to the right that we could reach. With screeching tires, we took off toward the road. The other two vehicles followed us. We drove through streets that no one knew and that were narrow enough for only one vehicle. We drove on sidewalks and any other means to get away from the rioting. We had no GPS and we all prayed that we weren't going in circles. Finally, we came across a road that one of us was familiar with. We found our way back to base.

Minister Shahrani kept his word. That evening, he met with the 300 mullahs and the riots were squelched.

Combat Stress and Trauma

The stress experienced in a combat zone is different than what we normally experience in the Western world. Psychologists and doctors have struggled to find a name that adequately describes the person who is deeply affected by the pile up of stressors. Berger presents several levels of stress, crisis, and trauma in the book, *Stress, Trauma, and Posttraumatic Growth: Social Context, Environment, and Identities* (2015). The following terms that Berger describes are an example of the shades of differences in meanings that the psychological community uses. While definitions of stress vary, Berger explains the concept of *stress* by identifying three core elements:

- First—"a situation occurs, which disrupts the usual stream of life and creates a state where the 'normal' way of doing things does not work or is insufficient"

- Second—"the situation is overtaxing because it demands resources that exceed those available for addressing it and thus a disparity is developed between the demands of the situation and the means for responding to it"

- Third—"whether the disparity is appraised by the exposed individual or system as strenuous, emotionally disruptive, endangering their well-being, and creating tension or as an opportunity for change and development. Stress is an ongoing process rather than a stable state." (p. 6)

Tension and emotional disruption are part of the development of stress. PTSD includes the term, *stress,* to encompass these concepts.

Berger explains that *distress* is hard to define but is "a combination of negative feelings of being easily annoyed or irritated, emotional pain, sadness, anxiety and fearfulness, and having uncontrollable temper outburst as a result of the subjective sense that something is wrong" (2015, p. 7). Distress explains the feelings that result from the stress event. *Crisis* has a broader definition in Berger's listings. Crisis is "a sharp or decisive change or life event which renders old patterns inadequate, with a resulting state of disorganization" (Berger, 2015, p. 7). A crisis generally lasts four to six weeks and involves the person questioning basic beliefs in life.

Trauma, according to Berger, is also difficult to define since the word is used to describe horrific, life-threatening events. The events, however, can take on differing levels of severity depending on the person using the word (Berger, 2015, p. 8). *Complex trauma* refers to "extended exposure to multiple simultaneous, sequential, or prolonged traumatic events, most often in the context of interpersonal relationships (such as intimate partner violence), placing the person at risk for severe health and mental health problems" (Berger, 2015, p. 9). *Retraumatization* can occur when traumatized individuals share the story of their trauma and are met by "reactions of disbelief, minimization, and pressure to keep it a secret and go on with life as if nothing happened" (Berger, 2015, p. 9). Thus, there are distinctions mainly in the degree of traumatization or in the length of time the reaction occurs.

Another type of traumatization, *secondary traumatization,* occurs with warriors and with family members. Therapists and others who provide care for warriors can begin to experience symptoms of secondary traumatization. Chaplains often experience secondary traumatization from their experiences listening to the traumatic experiences of the war fighters. They are the second highest professional group that experiences secondary traumatization on a regular basis. The military group that has the highest incidence of PTSD are the mortuary teams and others who care for the dead. Law enforcement officers, firefighters, disaster relief personnel, and emergency medical personnel deal with primary and secondary traumatization. Psychiatrists, psychologists, doctors, nurses, and therapists are other groups that experience secondary traumatization from their exposure to the stories of others and from their experience with the medical needs of warriors. Family members, particularly wives, can find themselves experiencing secondary traumatization from living with a traumatized warrior. The information we present below uses chaplain experiences to illustrate secondary traumatization. We also present information on spouses because these two groups are the ones to which we belong.

Berger explains how trauma indirectly impacts people via "intensive personal or professional relationships with direct victims." These symptoms include "compassion fatigue, secondary traumatic stress, vicarious effects, empathic strain, secondary traumatization, and co-victimization" (Berger, 2015, p. 10). People who have secondary traumatization identify with the direct victim's sufferings. In the case of chaplains, the number of direct victims that confide in them can produce the secondary traumatization (Berger, 2015, p. 10). Anyone who deals with direct victims of trauma is in an environment that can produce secondary traumatization.

Hoge explains some circumstances that can result in secondary traumatization as well as contribute to developing serious PTSD when warriors return from combat.

> These are situations in which warriors are unable to respond militarily, either because the enemy is elusive or because they're constrained by the rules of engagement (ROE). Rules of engagement are policies established by leaders in the war zone to protect civilian noncombatants, but warriors often feel hampered by them. (Hoge, 2010, p. 24)

Chaplains, as non-combatants, do not carry weapons at any time. Thus, they can find themselves traumatized when they are in the combat zone due to their extreme vulnerability.

Chaplains often experience feelings of vulnerability and feelings of intense exposure to the point that they feel defenseless. Under the Geneva Conventions, chaplains are considered non-combatants and, thus, do not carry weapons. Even though chaplains have assistants that provide personal security, chaplains can develop high levels of stress related to their inability to provide for their own personal physical security—Hoge's "warriors are unable to respond militarily" (2010, p. 24). These feelings of stress can lead to feelings of intense vulnerability. Dependency on others for security often causes high stress and intense vulnerability for chaplains, which also adds to the secondary traumatization. Chaplains choose to work in this warrior environment, but that choice does not offset the stress of being in combat or in a combat zone weaponless.

On one of my trips to Ramadi, Iraq, a chaplain stationed at Camp Blue Diamond asked to speak with me. As soon as we sat down to talk, he became highly agitated.

"I keep dreaming about them. Even when I'm awake, I see them…" he began before I could say anything.

"It's their teeth. That's all I see is their white teeth. I see their white teeth standing out from their charred bodies. I can't get it out of my mind" he said.

A few days before I arrived, this chaplain had been working to develop relationships with many of the Marines in the unit he was assigned to. The chaplain had really enjoyed talking with several of the Marines and was working to develop some activities to support them when they returned from going outside the wire. Two of the Marines, eager young men of about nineteen, had approached him the day before they went on patrol. Each had sat down with the chaplain to discuss some issues they had.

The next morning, these two Marines went on patrol. Later that afternoon, their command had asked this chaplain to identify the bodies of these two Marines who had been killed in their humvee when an IED exploded beside them. When he saw them, they were barely recognizable. Their bodies were burned and charred. Their teeth, however, stood out in stark whiteness.

Every time he closed his eyes, the chaplain saw the white teeth of those two young Marines. He was haunted by that memory. I listened as he told me his story as I had listened to chaplains all over Al Anbar Province relate their traumatic stories.

I kept hearing his voice and seeing him as he lowered his head into his hands and cried. I kept hearing, "All I see is their white teeth. All I see is their white teeth…." When I returned to Camp Fallujah, I began to dream about those white teeth in those charred bodies as well. That image haunted me in my dreams for many years.

I attended memorial services for those two Marines as I attended memorial services for each service member or civilian who died in the Al Anbar Province that year—112 in all. When I first arrived, it seemed that all I did was attend memorial services. I comforted the chaplains as they comforted their units. I comforted the Commanding Officers and Executive Officers. I found myself comforting those dealing with the dead so often that I felt locked in a merry-go-round. Everywhere I went there was death and dying.

As chaplains, we prayed with and for the units as they went on their missions. Then we prayed over the wounded when they returned. We also prayed over the dead and we prayed with the living. There was so much death and no time to grieve. We listened to the stories of those who lost buddies. We comforted those who were so numbed that they barely knew they needed comforting. So many young men and women the age of my sons were dying in gruesome ways. Like the Marines around me, I attended memorial services and then stuffed the grief inside as I returned to my duties. There was no time to deal with grief so we could only stuff it inside. We had to return to the living. I watched as other chaplains did the same thing.

During my tour in Iraq, I also visited the chaplains at the Theater Mortuary Evacuation Point (TMEP) at Kuwait City International Airport. When the military personnel who were killed-in-action (KIA) were evacuated from Iraq or Afghanistan, they went through the TMEP in Kuwait before being loaded on C17s headed for Dover Port Mortuary at Dover Air Force Base. Each day, the KIA flowed steadily through the TMEP in Kuwait.

I stood beside the chaplain assigned to the Theater Mortuary Evacuation Point and then joined him as he prayed for the dead. Each body transfer case was opened as the mortuary teams performed their duties of taking inventory of every item in the body transfer case. The chaplain working in the mortuary prayed over each body as the mortuary team completed its work. I stood beside the chaplain, praying with him, as he prayed over body after body after body. We stood in silent prayer as each body transfer case closed and then the mortuary team moved to the next body. Death and dying became my constant companions as I moved through the combat zone. I grew more and more numb as the days passed.

Proximity, Intensity, and Duration

Judith Herman (1997), whose work clarified many concepts of trauma, provides an explanation of traumatic experiences in the following:

> Traumatic events are extraordinary, not because they occur rarely, but rather because they overwhelm the ordinary human adaptations to life. Unlike commonplace misfortunes, traumatic events generally involve threats to life or bodily integrity, or a close personal encounter with violence and death. They confront human beings with the extremities of helplessness and terror, and evoke the responses of catastrophe....[T]he common denominator of psychological trauma is a feeling of "intense fear,

helplessness, loss of control, and threat of annihilation." (p. 33)

The level of trauma that warriors experience in the combat zone includes intense fear and intense threat of annihilation.

The day was hot and sunny like every other day at Camp Fallujah, Iraq, during the late spring of 2007. My job as Force Chaplain for II Marine Expeditionary Force included visiting chaplains located throughout Al Anbar Province, Iraq. On this day, I was traveling with the Force Commanding General, his Aid-de-Camp, and my RP (Religious Program Specialist) aboard a CH-46 Sea Knight Helicopter. Two AH-1 W Cobra gunships would be escorting another CH-46 and us over the Saqlawiyah region and into Ramadi, Iraq. The Saqlawiyah region was an area where, on 7 February 2007, insurgents had shot down a CH-46, killing all seven aboard. Our route passed over several areas known as hotbeds of enemy activity.

As we flew toward Ramadi, the helicopter violently pitched ninety degrees to the portside. I heard three loud boom, boom, booms! I gripped the aluminum frame of my seat to steady myself. As I looked across the helicopter and out of the window, I saw the ground racing toward me where sky should be. I gripped harder as I realized that we were dropping from the sky. I looked down at the General and his Aid-de-Camp as they were gripping their seats and grasping what was happening.

The helicopter continued making violent rolls as we were falling, jinking, turning, and diving to evade the electronic signal that had locked onto our helicopter. The violent maneuvers continued as the pilot flew evasive moves. I saw the ground continuing to race toward us.

Suddenly, at about 100 feet off the ground, the pilot was able to level out the helicopter. We skimmed the nap of the earth as we covered the distance to Camp Ramadi. As we entered the airfield, the pilot rapidly flared the nose of the helicopter and sat the aircraft down with a solid landing. Relief flooded through the helicopter as we realized we were on solid ground.

Trauma, as we will use it in this book, is the occurrences within the combat zone that cause stress and the pile up of stressors and that have "proximity, intensity, and duration" (Meadors & Lamson, 2008, p. 25). The intensity, fear, helplessness, loss of control, and threat of annihilation are also key components with our concept of trauma. Many sources discuss how stress affects the mind and body, but few enter the spiritual realm. Herman describes the "ordinary human response to danger" as a highly complex "integrated system of reactions, encompassing both body and mind" (1997, p. 34). She does not refer to the spiritual side of traumatization. Calhoun and Tedeschi advise counselors to stay neutral in terms of religion when counseling clients who have experienced trauma (2013, p. 130). This exclusion of the entire person—mind, body, and spirit—has omitted a fundamental part of the total being of a warrior. Thus, healing is thwarted or avoided because of the resistance to discuss the spiritual wound, also called *moral injury*, that warriors experience.

Peter Marin's work with veterans returning from the Vietnam War is the basis for his article, "Living in Moral Pain," in which he discusses the limits of psychology for dealing with trauma and its aftermath. He presents "the inadequacy of psychological categories and language in describing the nature and pain of human conscience" (1981, p. 74). Marin continues by explaining how therapists and patients approach therapy:

> Our great therapeutic dream in America is that the past is escapable, that suffering can be avoided, that happiness is always possible, and that insight inevitably leads to joy. But life's lessons—so much more apparent in literature than in therapy—teach us something else again, something that is both true of, and applicable to, the experience of the vets. Try as they do to escape it, the past pursues them; the closer they come to the truth of

their acts, the more troubled they are, the more apart they find themselves, and the more tragic becomes their view of life. (1981, p. 74).

Trauma affects the body by many responses, the mind by dreams and chaos, and the spirit by a woundedness that psychology generally does not address.

Trauma's Effects on the Body and Mind

Separating trauma's effects on the body from its effects on the mind is difficult. Some reactions begin in the mind but are carried out in the body in a highly complex system of reactions. Herman describes trauma's effects on the body and mind by stating that threat:

- "Initially arouses the sympathetic nervous system, causing the person in danger to feel an adrenalin rush and go into a state of alert"

- "Concentrates a person's attention on the immediate situation"

- "Alters ordinary perceptions: people in danger are often able to disregard hunger, fatigue, or pain"

- "Evokes intense feelings of fear and anger" (1997, p. 34)

These reactions are normal and adaptive as the threatened person mobilizes for strenuous action, either in combat or in flight.

Herman discusses how a traumatized person reacts when actions produce little or no results. The traumatic situation and the threat do not change; thus, the threatened person begins to exist within the traumatized state of being.

> Traumatic reactions occur when action is of no avail. When neither resistance nor escape is possible, the human system of self-defense becomes overwhelmed and disorganized. Each component of the ordinary response to danger, having lost its utility, tends to persist in an altered and exaggerated state long after the actual danger is over. Traumatic events produce profound and lasting changes in physiological arousal, emotion, cognition, and memory. Moreover, traumatic events may sever these normally integrated functions from one another. The traumatized person may experience intense emotion but without clear memory of the event, or may remember everything in detail but without emotion. She may find herself in a constant state of vigilance and irritability without knowing why. Traumatic symptoms have a tendency to become disconnected from their source and to take on a life of their own. (Herman, 1997, p. 34)

The changes that occur within traumatized persons during prolonged stress events can cause the people to separate feelings and reactions that normally are paired together within their minds and bodies. This separation of the feelings and reactions from the event or memory can cause these persons to react as though they are constantly in danger, but they don't understand their reactions.

War affects warriors in this way and in ways distinct from the civilian population. Hoge explains the warrior's mind and body responses to threats in the combat zones. Clarifying the distinction between trauma in combat zones and trauma in civilian settings, Hoge explains that most civilian trauma is a single event that the civilians are unprepared for while warriors encounter "potentially" dangerous or traumatic events daily or multiple times a day. Hoge states,

> What distinguishes traumatic events for warriors is their preparation and the fact that they might experience

> multiple events in the course of their professional duties... Warriors may still be surprised or devastated when combat events occur, but they have an understanding that these things will likely happen, and have prepared for them to the best of their ability. (Hoge, 2010, pp. 20-21)

Because warriors are more prepared for trauma than most of society, they often are surprised that they can be traumatized by the events in the combat zone. Thus, admitting that they are traumatized is more difficult for them.

> Warriors experience effects from working every day under constant threat of attack or ambush, even if nothing happens; long periods of boredom and waiting can be punctuated by bursts of insanity. Environmental stressors (heat, cold, carrying heavy loads), exhaustion, and sleep deprivation magnify the impact that these experiences have. (Hoge, 2010, p. 20)

Hoge continues by stating that trauma in combat zones is not just taking direct or indirect fire, but it also includes:

> ...experiencing a near miss on one's life; knowing someone who was seriously injured or killed; handling body parts; witnessing or being involved in accidents involving vehicles or aircraft; witnessing noncombatants suffering; or seeing poverty, pain, destruction, or ethnic violence. Some events are so catastrophic that there isn't anything that compares, especially losing a close buddy, but there are also cumulative effects from multiple less severe incidents. (Hoge, 2010, p. 20)

Thus, Hoge concludes, warriors' have stressors that lead to PTSD that differ from the model currently used that is "conceptualized around a single traumatic event, although warriors routinely experience multiple events" (2010, p. 21). The current diagnostic models don't consider that multiple events traumatize warriors. Therefore, these models are lacking in another area besides the lack of treating the entirety of a person—mind, body, and spirit.

I *always* placed my gear in *exactly* the same place when I went to bed. Many nights I would be startled awake by the sirens announcing incoming rockets or small arms fire. I had to be able to throw on my gear and get to the shelters in a matter of seconds. I never knew when an attack would come so I was always prepared. I can't count the number of times that I ran for the shelter in the middle of the night, grabbing my gear in the dark as I sprinted out the door heading for my bunker.

I also became adept at cleaning out humvees. The Deputy Force Chaplain and I had ready kits by our feet no matter where we were. If we were in our office, the ready kits were by our feet. If we were in the chow hall, the ready kits were there as well. We took them to services in the chapels. We always had them with us. When we would hear the thump-thump of helicopters or the roar of humvees, we would grab our bags and run to the vehicles. We would help offload the wounded and then, if time permitted, we would clean out the humvees. Blood would pool everywhere but we would scrub the blood until the vehicle was usable again. Some days, the wounded poured back to base. Blood was everywhere.

This daily up-tempo lifestyle that contains varieties of stressors, stressful incidents, and threats of stressful incidents leads warriors to develop certain types of reactions. These reactions are part of their training, but the life and death situations in the combat zones require warriors to fine-tune these reactions. The goal of the warriors is to survive whatever threats are present and to return home. In order to do this, warriors fine-tune different aspects of their bodies, their emotions, and their reactions. These areas include:

- **Focus:** Depending on the danger, warriors may use a scanning focus to detect threats which requires their minds to jump from thing to thing, never settling on one item for very long; a tunnel-vision focus on the thing that they think is the greatest threat; and a wide relaxed focus that focuses on a certain threat but also uses the peripheral vision to scan for threats (Hoge, 2010, pp. 93-94).

- **Sleep:** Historically, military leaders have considered four hours of sleep in the combat zone as acceptable. Most operations occur at night so this short sleep cycle can be even shorter. The body doesn't rest as well in the day as it does at night. Sleep deprivation is a major issue for warriors (Hoge, 2010, pp. 56-58).

- **Situational Awareness:** "During times of stress and danger, the body is revved up due to adrenaline and other chemicals; the heart rate is increased, breathing becomes more rapid and shallow, muscle tension increases, and the mind becomes hyperalert. As a result, warriors are able to maintain high situational awareness, which is a very useful skill. This includes

    - "Scanning the environment for anything that might be a threat,

    - "Using their own fear or anxiety as a warning signal, and

    - "Ensuring that there are always escape routes" (Hoge, 2010, p. 58).

- **Control and Reflexive Actions:** Control is essential to surviving in the combat zone. If warriors react too slowly or with the wrong sequence of events under fire, then their chances of survival lessen. Warriors depend on

- Their equipment
- Their training
- Their buddies.

If any one of these three fail, then the mission could fail as well. The key for survival requires warriors to

- Have all equipment in the best working order *exactly* where it should be,

- Do *exactly* what is required based on their training when warriors are under fire

- Rely on buddies to do *exactly* what is required of them each time (Hoge, 2010, pp. 59-60).

"The success of the mission and the ability to respond to enemy contact in a flexible and effective way requires that everyone on the team perform their tasks instantly and in the correct way, according to their training and experience" (Hoge, 2010, p. 60). This training for being under fire starts with each team member memorizing common tasks, which, after intensive training, become reflective actions (Hoge, 2010, p. 60). Thus, the coordination of a well-trained team is essential to survival in the combat zone.

- **Brain:** Two parts of the brain that usually work in harmony are the limbic system and the medial prefrontal cortex.

- The *limbic system* is the flight-or-fight area of the brain. This area works as an alarm system in times of high threat to set off various reactions throughout the body that include heightened "heart rate, blood pressure, circulation, breathing, and hormone balance (e.g., adrenaline and the stress hormone, cortisol)" (Hoge, 2010, p. 54). This alarm system causes the release of adrenaline that "tenses muscles; increases alertness, attention, heart rate, and blood pressure; and changes the way a person scans the environment for threats" (Hoge, 2010, p. 55).

  The limbic system's primary emotion is anger. Fear is the second emotion but warriors, through their training, control the fear with anger. "The limbic alarm system of the brain 'hijacks' the conscious rational areas in order to ensure that the person's entire attention and focus is directed toward survival" (Hoge, 2010, p. 55). Warriors have no control over this function of the brain. "The reflexes honed during military training and combat are some of the strongest reflexes that a person can ever develop—reflexes that become a way of life for a warrior" (Hoge, 2010, p. 55).

- The *medial prefrontal cortex* is located in the brain in front of the limbic system. The medial prefrontal cortex works with the limbic area, controlling the fight-or-flight reflex. It helps determine if the threat is real or imagined and thus, if the limbic system should sound an alarm to the body. "The medial prefrontal cortex is critical in planning, decision-making, and thinking through actions. It's important for anticipating what you're going to do next and thinking through the sequence of things" (Hoge, 2010, p. 56).

- ○ "In summary, the limbic system ensures that you can react immediately to threat, and the medial prefrontal cortex helps to keep this in balance" (Hoge, 2010, p. 56). The limbic system, however, becomes the controlling system in the combat zone.

- **Limited Emotions:** Anger is the dominant emotion in the up-tempo environment of the combat zone. The other common emotion is feeling no emotion at all, a numbing of emotions or detachment during periods of extreme stress. Anger is the dominant emotion of the fight-or-flight part of the brain during high stress times.

Anger masks other emotions, such as fear or sadness, allowing the warrior to do what needs to be done under fire. Even if a unit loses a team member, right after the casualty is removed or the memorial service is finished, the grief has to be put on hold when the unit goes back "outside the wire" (Hoge, 2010, p. 59).

Warriors rely on their training, their buddies, and seasoned warriors to help them control their anger. In that way, anger doesn't take over and hamper the missions. Hoge adds, "After coming out of a combat environment, it can take a long time before a warrior can express a full range of emotions again" (2010, p. 59).

- **Cognitive Problems:** Memory, attention, and concentration all are focused on survival in the combat zones. Warriors use essential survival skills to maintain control under fire. Memory, attention, and concentration all become oriented toward survival with few other issues entering the warriors' minds. The intensity of the focus on survival can interfere with the broadening of issues when the warrior returns (Hoge, 2010, p. 59).

- **Reaction Times:** As humans, we are always responding physiologically and emotionally to stressors and non-stressors within our environments. We have feelings whether or not we are aware of them. An event occurs, we process the event, and we respond by a reaction. For example, at a baseball field, we hear "Heads up!" and everyone ducks and covers their heads. For warriors, "combat experiences tend to shorten the time between stressful events and behaviors. Warriors often have hair-trigger reactions to stressful situations, and this can lead to behaviors they later regret. A stressful event may automatically result in an action without paying any attention to the feelings or thoughts inside" (Hoge, 2010, p. 89). Warriors respond to "Heads up!" by hitting the ground and rolling under the bleacher. Little to no thought goes into the correct action. Warriors responded automatically because of their training and combat experience. This quick responsiveness is often what saves the warriors' lives.

- **Physiological Reactions:** Physiological reactions are intuitive reactions based on warriors' training, knowledge, and experience. Combat teaches warriors the following:

- To become highly attuned to any physiological warning signs of anxiety or danger, such as hearts suddenly starting to race; breath quickening; hair standing on end; and neck, chest, or upper back tensing.

- Changes in alertness, mental attention, muscle tension, heart rate, and general anxiety are part of the warriors' reactions to threats (Hoge, 2010, pp. 89-90).

- **Fear:** Warriors are trained in how to respond to threat and danger, and how to handle high anxiety, stress, and fear. Anxiety usually is the outward manifestation of fear; however, warriors perceive and react to fear differently than an untrained person. "Warriors understand how to use fear to their advantage, to tune into their level of fear as a warning signal, and then to dial-up or down their level of alertness, tension, and awareness of potential threats.... Warriors don't talk much about being helpless or paralyzed by fear, but instead about how their training helps them to function effectively in the face of fear. Fear becomes almost a sixth sense" (Hoge, 2010, p. 90).

The up-tempo pace of the combat zone causes warriors to fine-tune their survival skills. These skills affect warriors' minds and bodies as they respond to the intense atmosphere of constant threat. The trauma, however, also affects the spirits of those warriors who endure the combat zone.

My daily life in Iraq was much more intense than in Afghanistan. When I arrived the area was very "hot," meaning that many firefights and battles were being fought. The death toll was high and, as chaplains, we listened to story after story of these combat situations. As the II MEF Chaplain, I was responsible for all of the chaplains in the Al Anbar Province. Many of these chaplains needed someone to listen to their stories of the traumatic situations they listened to and that they experienced. My deputy and I traveled the Province listening to these chaplains and listening to the Marines who were in the middle of the firefights. We heard story after story of events that had traumatized the Marines, sailors, and chaplains.

Every moment of every day was a possible moment for an attack—rockets or otherwise. Up-tempo intensity was the pace of our lives as we worked to stay alive to return home. The importance of equipment in working condition and always placed in exactly the same place is a major element in my survival. We raced to our destinations, constantly looking for IED's and shooters. We lived in a state of intense situational awareness—anyone or anything could bring death to us. The combat zone was a place where we were constantly aware of how fragile life is.

Trauma's Effects on the Spirit

Trauma affects warriors' minds and bodies but the deepest effect is on the spirits of warriors. This less examined aspect of our lives as humans exists as a major wound for warriors. Robert Grant, in *The Way of the Wound*, notes that many doctors and psychologists often minimize not only the "existence and impact of psychological trauma, but the spiritual dimensions of trauma as well" (1996, p. 6). Grant describes trauma in the following:

> Trauma is not just an event but a constellation of meanings and relationships. Side effects, fears, betrayals, losses of innocence, failures to be understood and the reorganisation of beliefs are all part of the trauma constellation. Trauma demands a change of visions. Trauma stirs the deeper mind. It activates a profound questioning that differentiates humans from all other forms of life. Trauma is an invitation to change and to pass

through the deepest centre of one's nature and come out on the other side. (1996, p. 38)

Trauma survivors seek deeper meanings for life, including questioning long held beliefs about God and life.

Grant explains that "[t]rauma is an invitation onto the spiritual path. Illness is a refusal to embrace the meanings that accompany this invitation. Healing requires an expansion of meaning. An inability or reluctance to seek wholeness and greater connectiveness lies at the root of most psychological and spiritual problems" (Grant, 1996, p. 38). Trauma is the human journey in its most intense form; thus, a "spirituality of trauma feeds the hungry souls of victims and helps them discover or rediscover the best aspects of their spiritual traditions while reframing what traditional psychology refers to as the 'pathological'" (Grant, 1996, p. x). The after-effects of war affect the mind, body, and spirit of warriors. Ignoring the spiritual traumatization treats only two-thirds of the person. Trauma is part of life that leads to growth. Treating it as a mental illness can prevent that growth.

An article, "Spirituality and Readjustment Following Warzone Experiences," discusses several effects that trauma has on people who believe in God. Trauma raises questions about the nature of God, His involvement with people, and the problem of evil. The basic question of "If God is all-powerful and God is all-good, how does God allow evil to exist in the world?" (Drescher et al., 2007, p. 295). Spirituality, however, requires the traumatized person to respond to God through the Holy Spirit. It is not a battle to understand God, but, instead, is a call to a journey that goes through the trauma and the wound to find one's authentic self.

The authentic self is the person that God created us to be. As we mature, we begin to change our authentic self as we adapt to expectations from our families, our peers, our schools, our jobs, and other influences in our lives. Trauma breaks those false images and leaves the traumatized person without any of the former means of facing life. The traumatized person views these former means as false because those means could not protect the person from trauma. In this state, the Holy Spirit is able to reach the authentic person that has, to that point, been hidden behind the trappings of the false self.

In the five months between Afghanistan and Iraq, I traveled to Landstuhl, Germany, to visit the Landstuhl Regional Medical Center in order to understand the journey that our wounded Marines would take as they left Iraq. I met the chaplains in the hospital and was touring the building when one chaplain asked me if I wanted to meet the bus that was bringing the wounded over from Ramstein Air Force Base. These wounded had left Iraq that morning. I agreed and we went outside to meet the bus.

As they began to move the wounded from the bus, a chaplain asked if I wanted to pray with the wounded Marine who was next in line to leave the bus. I prayed for him and then helped move him to the gurney. I prayed for and helped with several more men. The last man I helped with was a Lance Corporal. I had not encountered anyone whose wounds were so severe. Both hands were wrapped in bandages. As my eyes ran down his body, I saw bloody bandages in several areas. His body stopped at the top of his legs. He had both hands but had lost both legs. I prayed for this Marine and helped move him to a gurney.

The Marine was moved to intensive care and I went by later that day to check on him and to pray for him. The next day, I visited him again and prayed for him. By the following day, he was awake but groggy and had the breathing tube out of his throat. When I entered his room, he looked at me and said that he remembered me. He said he remembered me praying for him and he thanked me for it. One of his hands was no longer bandaged. He wrote me notes.

In one of the notes, he asked me how long it would be before he could get back to his friends and fight again. I looked at this young man of nineteen or twenty and saw fierce determination in his face. I told him that his friends had not made it out of the humvee. I also knew he would never fight again without his legs.

As tears ran down his face, I reached out and placed my hand on his shoulder. I stood like that for awhile, saying nothing. After awhile, he reached up and squeezed my hand as the tears ran down his face.

I felt such an intense pride in this young man. He had sacrificed much, but his concern was for his buddies. Tears ran down my face that day as well. Before I left, I prayed with him again. I have dreamed of this young Marine in battle, losing his legs, and screaming in pain. He became part of my dreams as the first of many severely wounded that I prayed over and prayed with.

Grant develops the concept of spirituality as the essence of this journey through the wound. The authentic self is able, with the help of the Holy Spirit, to engage the wound and journey through that wound.

> The task of every trauma victim is to discover healing and direction in events that not only injure but which have the power to destroy. How to develop hope and spiritual deepening in the midst of despair is a challenge that every survivor must meet. Most humans experience some form of trauma during the course of their lives. Life, in the final analysis, is forever on the verge of overwhelming one's capacities to cope. Traumatic injuries, along with other wounds, are not accidents. They are catalysts that have the potential to place one on the spiritual path. (Grant, 1997, p. 3)

Our modern Western life fills every moment with activity or sound. With the constant presence of phones, music, and television, we leave little to no space to hear the voice of God. Our attention is always focused, leaving no space for the Holy Spirit to guide us. Thus, trauma has become "one common experiential ground through which the Spirit is currently trying to make Itself known. Profound realisations and unsettling questions, carried by every victim of trauma, are typically disowned and, by necessity, overlooked by mainstream consciousness" (Grant, 1997, p. 6). Trauma is a means for us to understand the deeper meanings and to obtain a deeper relationship with God.

Few people, however, choose the path toward spiritual healing because it is a difficult and painful path. Many victims of trauma choose to hide their pain in addictions in order to dull the pain of knowing the truths that their wounds exposed. Those truths include the concepts that the protections they had previously developed are not able to protect them from the trauma that life throws at them. Those warriors who are willing to take the path toward healing "inspire the rest of humanity to keep reaching for wholeness and the Spirit. Choosing the path of healing requires that victims stretch themselves on the cross of trauma in order to discover that their essence is not something that can be defined by any possession, relationship or image of self" (Grant, 1997, pp. 6-7). Stretching onto a cross of trauma is not an image that I embraced even though I knew that Jesus encourages us to "take up your cross daily and follow Me" (Matthew 16: 24).

This journey from uncovering my authentic self to spiritual healing by the Holy Spirit is the one that I traveled to find hope and peace. Using Hoge's up-tempo concepts, Kathy began to understand my interactions with the family. Through her understanding, I was able to begin to feel safe within our home. That safety allowed me then to be able to seek the Holy Spirit's guidance as I began the difficult journey to uncover my authentic self. This story is what the last half of this book relates. We will begin with the Holy Spirit brooding over the dark chaos in our minds affected by PTSD.

CHAPTER SIX

"Most Holy Spirit Who Didst Brood Upon the Chaos Dark and Rude"

Post Traumatic Stress Disorder (PTSD) is the diagnosis that applies to warriors who have difficulties readjusting when they return from the combat zone. The terms have much broader usage, applying to anyone who struggles with the aftermath of trauma. In this chapter, I will explain how I began to learn about PTSD so that I could somehow help Mike and in so doing, help my family. I was unaware of the studies in positive psychology and in Posttraumatic Growth (PTG) in 2006 when I began researching PTSD. I found that I understood PTSD descriptive language, but I didn't have any practical knowledge to apply to our lives.

Intensity, Severity, and Duration

Richard Tedeschi and Lawrence Calhoun (2004) describe PTSD symptoms as falling into three distinct categories that they term: physical reactions, psychological reactions, and emotional reactions. Physical reactions to high levels of stress include fatigue, muscle tension and aches, gastric symptoms, and general physical discomfort. Psychological reactions to major life crises include distressing and dysfunctional patterns of thinking, disbelief, psychological numbness, and repetitive intrusive thoughts and images that are unpleasant and distressing. The authors categorize emotions that people can experience in response to a major life crisis as sadness, depression, guilt, anger, and general irritability. They distinguish specific fears that accompany emotions for sets of circumstances that "threaten the person's physical well-being, anxiety or specific fears are common. Depending on the intensity, severity, and duration of physical threat or suffering (either direct or vicarious), the anxious responses can persist for a long time after the actual threat is removed" (Tedeschi & Calhoun, 2004, p. 2). These sets of symptoms are common to warriors who return from the battle zones; however, Tedeschi and Calhoun's descriptions are not inclusive of effects to the spirit.

Hoge discusses the reality of the PTSD definitions in the DSM (*Diagnostic and Statistical Manual of Mental Disorders*) by stating, "We don't have any definitive means of making a mental disorder diagnosis other than what patients tell us about their symptoms" (2010, p. 7) which mental health specialists then compare to the DSM. Hoge stresses that the DSM has its uses, but it does not provide the same quality of descriptions that a manual on physical diseases provides. Many of the symptoms in the DSM overlap with each other (Hoge, 2010, p. 7).

PTSD, however, is unique because the diagnosis is tied to trauma in some way. If a list of symptoms make their appearance after a traumatic event(s), then the diagnosis is often PTSD. The PTSD diagnosis is largely based on trauma in civilian settings. "This is very different than the experiences of warriors who are trained to encounter trauma as part of their profession" (Hoge, 2010, pp. 7, 9). Warriors must understand that they are experiencing *reactions* to the combat zone and that they don't necessarily have a *disorder*. Hoge stresses that every symptom of PTSD "stems from things your body normally does in response to severe danger or stress" (2010, pp. 9, 11). Thus, what is normal in combat is abnormal when warriors return home.

Historical Approaches

"One of the many casualties of the war's devastation was the illusion of manly honor and glory in battle," states Judith Herman (1997, p. 20) in referring to World War I veterans. This statement, however, can apply to wars much earlier in our country's history with the effects of the Revolutionary War and the Civil War shaping the concept of honor and glory in battle as well. "Soldier's heart" was coined to refer to men with PTSD symptoms in early wars. In World War I, the term, "shell shock," referred to men with PTSD symptoms. Shell shock was thought to be a physical ailment; however, by World War II, the psychiatrists began studying the effects of combat on men in order to determine how much rest warriors needed before they could return to the fighting. What these psychiatrists discovered was "that *any* man could break down under fire and that psychiatric casualties could be predicted in direct proportion to the severity of combat exposure" (Herman, 1997, pp. 20-25). Therefore, warriors shouldn't feel shame because they are traumatized due to duration or intensity of exposure in the combat zone.

In 1946, J. W. Appel and G. W. Beebe concluded that even the strongest soldiers could be broken with 200-240 days of combat. "There is no such thing as 'getting used to combat.'... Each moment of combat imposes a strain so great that men will break down in direct relation to the intensity and duration of their exposure. Thus psychiatric casualties are as inevitable as gunshot and shrapnel wounds in warfare" (Herman, 1997, p. 25). The psychiatrists and psychologists in post-World War II research asserted that the best protection against PTSD symptoms for soldiers is the bond that develops in the small fighting group. Roy Grinker and John Spiegel argued: "The effect of combat...is not like the writing on a slate that can be erased, leaving the slate as it was before. Combat leaves a lasting impression on men's minds, changing them as radically as any crucial experience through which they live" (Herman, 1997, p. 26). Warriors are changed by combat and can't expect to return to "normal" when they come home nor should others have that expectation of them.

Danger's Effects on the Mind and Body

When warriors return home from a combat deployment, they often feel that they are "returning to the three-dimensional world after experiencing a fourth dimension. It's hard to sort out who is really crazy—you, or the rest of the world. The rest of the world can't comprehend the concept of a fourth dimension; they can't relate to it, and may not even be interested" (Hoge, 2010, p. xiv). Thus, warriors can feel they are wasting their time dealing with people who can't understand the experiences they have had. This frustration builds within returned warriors and they find themselves wishing to return to the "known world" of combat.

Hoge discusses the ways that the military has approached sending warriors back to the combat zone during the Iraq and Afghanistan wars. He remarks:

> In recent years the military has considered the "resetting" of a warrior's health after combat in much the same way that it considers the resetting or refitting of equipment and vehicles. The protracted duration of the Iraq and Afghanistan wars and the reality of multiple deployments have led to the unrealistic expectation that warriors (and their family members) can "reset" physically and mentally for another combat tour in less than twelve months. (Hoge, 2010, p. xvii)

Warriors, as we have experienced, are not able to be "reset" like equipment. Mike had about two weeks between the time he returned from Afghanistan until he reported for duty with 2D MEF to begin war preparations with them. He had only six months between Afghanistan and Iraq. This information led me to begin understanding the reasons for Mike's changes.

Responding to danger is a complex, integrated systems of reactions that encompass the totality of a warrior's mind and body. The changes in arousal, attention, perception, and emotion are normal, adaptive reactions. These reactions mobilize the threatened person for strenuous action, either in battle or in flight. Threat does the following to people:

- Arouses the sympathetic nervous system so that an adrenaline rush occurs

- Alters ordinary perceptions (hunger, fatigue, and pain can be ignored)

- Concentrates attention on the immediate situation

- Evokes intense feelings of fear and anger. (Herman, 1997, p. 34)

Thus, threat produces physical and emotional changes within warriors.

The problem with danger is that in the combat zone, action often doesn't prevent the traumatic experiences. Herman explains the response to danger when actions are pointless against it in the following:

> When neither resistance nor escape is possible, the human system of self-defense becomes overwhelmed and disorganized. Each component of the ordinary response to danger, having lost its utility, tends to persist in an altered and exaggerated state long after the actual danger is over. Traumatic events produce profound and lasting changes in physiological arousal, emotion, cognition, and memory. Moreover, traumatic events may sever these normally integrated functions from one another. The traumatized person may experience intense emotion

> but without clear memory of the event, or may remember everything in detail but without emotion. She may find herself in a constant state of vigilance and irritability without knowing why. Traumatic symptoms have a tendency to become disconnected from their source and to take on a life of their own. (1997, p. 34)

Repeated exposure to the traumatic events can cause the traumatic symptoms to become disconnected in the traumatized person's mind and body. Often, traumatized people are unaware that this fragmentation has occurred because they have existed in this state for a long time while they were in the combat zone. Herman concludes, "This kind of fragmentation, whereby trauma tears apart a complex system of self-protection that normally functions in an integrated fashion, is central to the historic observations on post-traumatic stress disorder" (Herman, 1997, p. 34). This fragmentation can't be reset easily.

I was beginning to understand what PTSD was. The fragmentation of the person exposed to trauma and the disconnection of responses from the continual exposure to danger and threat described Mike precisely. These elements had come home with Mike, but I didn't lose focus on the fact that Mike was home. There was no danger here. There was no threat here. What was I supposed to *do* to counter these symptoms? My desire was for my husband to find some relief from the nightmares and from the continual feelings of being threatened. I could not find a way to move him from where he was to a place that was more peace-filled. I found some more sources to read.

Existential Existence

Some of my readings from earlier in my life came to mind as I was trying to find ways to reach out to my husband. Now I know that these books came to mind through the Holy Spirit's direction. God was answering my prayers bit by bit. Robert Grant's *The Way of the Wound* echoed the books that described the warriors' return as difficult with warriors being unable—and unwilling—to fit back into the society that they left. Grant explains that humans are always in the process of becoming, but most people "have strong desires to maintain current understandings of self. Their wish is to dam the incessant flow of becoming and design a once-and-for-all version of self" (Grant, 1996, p. 17). Our understandings of our self are "forever tentative and therefore never final." We understand ourselves through internal and external realities which form systems of meaning. These meanings are formed by family, friends, church, business associates, and others who operate in our worlds. These groups work to provide "socially dictated versions" of who we are (Grant, 1996, p. 17). Thus, when a warrior returns with a different reality and different meanings for existence, the social groups that the warrior left quite often reject the different person and long for and cling to images from the past. This longing can be expressed through statements such as "I just want my husband back" or "I want life to be normal again." The warrior often no longer remembers who that person was. Grant explains this conflict of approaches as follows: "Most people prefer life to be neat, calm and orderly like their neighbourhoods. Whereas trauma loves to run wild in suburban consciousness" (Grant, 1996, p. 25). Trauma produces radical changes within warriors that leaves them unable to accept what was "normal" before their exposure to the combat zone.

Henri Nouwen's *The Wounded Healer* is another book that has provided me with great insights at several points in my life. I turned back to this book and found that Nouwen described the warrior's predicament when that warrior returns to America from combat. Nouwen develops this concept with: "[The warrior] is a man who has lost naïve faith in the possibilities of technology and is painfully aware that the same powers that enable man to create new life styles carry the potential for self-destruction" (1972, p. 5). He continues by describing the people around us. "When we look around us we see man paralyzed by dislocation and fragmentation, caught in the prison of his own mortality" (Nouwen, 1972, p. 15). Warriors come home with an awareness of their own mortality, having faced it numerous times a day in the combat zone. Nouwen's descriptions of the "nuclear man" of the 1960s and 1970s resonates with the descriptions of the warrior's place in our society today. Nouwen presents this concept for people struggling to make sense of the world: "A man confronted with all this and trying to make sense of it cannot possibly deceive himself with one idea, concept, or thought system which could bring these contrasting images together into one consistent outlook on life" (1972, p. 11). Nouwen's writings echo many of the PTSD sources that spoke of warriors' inability to adapt to "normal" life or to believe in the "old" belief systems that Americans cling to.

My struggle was that my husband understood all of this about combat and PTSD; yet, he still was struggling with so much inside of his head and spirit. My reading was providing me with information, but it did not provide me with any kind of answer to my question of "How can I help him?"

PTSD Descriptions

Many definitions that I read defined PTSD similar to this description:

> By its nature, this is a disorder that puts tremendous difficulties in the way of the injured veteran's personal relations and functioning. The avoidance symptoms of psychic numbing, withdrawal, detachment, constricted affect, and loss of interest in previously enjoyed activities are symptoms that undermine the individual's ability to maintain the intimacy of family life. The hyper arousal symptoms include heightened irritability and hostility, which would make it difficult for the afflicted veteran to control his aggression. (Dekel & Solomon, 2007, p. 138).

Again, I understood this definition and I saw how it could fit, but what could be done to help?

Calhoun and Tedeschi summarize the negative side of PTSD. Distressing emotions that PTSD brings can include anxiety, fear, distress (varying degrees), sadness, guilt, anger, irritability, and depression. Distressing thoughts and images such as memories of traumatic events are constantly present. Some of the problematic behaviors that are part of PTSD include misuse of alcohol, drugs, or tobacco; excessive use of food; increase in aggressive behaviors; physical problems; and psychological problems. The physical activation, "fight-or-flight," is easily triggered and can last for awhile (Calhoun & Tedeschi, 2013, pp. 1-5).

Mike witnessed and counseled countless numbers of men and women in the combat zone and home from the combat zone who use pornography and sex as adaptive behaviors. The numbing of the mind and spirit with the intense focus of sex is another problematic behavior that warriors engage in to numb their pain. Often, the momentary blocking of reality through sexual pleasure is followed by tremendous guilt that only exacerbates the adjustment issues of warriors.

I found other sources that were less than helpful. Some books and articles focused on the spiritual side of the wound and suggested that this war wound was actually the devil in our homes. Some other advice was that wives needed to wake every morning, don their spiritual warfare gear, and prepare for battle against their wounded husbands. I was appalled at some of these suggestions. Some advice suggested that wives were at war with their husbands—a spiritual war—and that our "war" was equal to what our husbands had experienced in the combat zone. This approach echoed the concept that people at home do not understand what happens in the combat zone. I felt so frustrated and alone as I sought answers. I continued to pray for God to change Mike and to make him listen to me. I continued to watch my husband's struggle and I grew frustrated with my inability to find any relief for him.

Beginnings

Mike returned from Iraq in 2008. In 2011, he began therapy for the second time during the summer after he retired. During those three years, we struggled to communicate, to pray, to engage each other. Nothing seemed to work for either of us. During the second round of therapy, Mike's counselor gave him a book by Dr. Charles Hoge entitled *Once a Warrior Always a Warrior: Navigating the Transition from Combat to Home*, which became the key to my understanding what was happening with Mike. I had tried to take in all the concepts, but I didn't know how to apply them. Dr. Hoge's book opened the communication channels between us again.

Hoge explains what skills are needed for combat and how those same skills appear in warriors at home. Hoge begins by defining the type of warrior who develops PTSD. He writes:

> [T]he development of PTSD after combat experiences has very little (or nothing) to do with the character, upbringing, or genetics of the warrior. What remains is that certain events are profoundly devastating and have a much stronger impact neurologically than others, a situation that the warrior has absolutely no control over. PTSD in these situations represents normal reactions to extremely abnormal (or extraordinary) events. (Hoge, 2010, p. 28).

I had already rationalized the concept that war is the kind of experience that changes anyone. What would a person be like if they went to war and suffered no change? But Hoge's concept that nothing protects warriors from the horrors of war and that PTSD is a normal reaction to those events was one that resonated deeply with me.

Hoge's explanations of the experiences of combat and the skills required was the information that most affected my approach to my husband. Hoge explains, "These warriors were continuing to feel physically revved up and hyperalert after returning home. They were reacting to situations back home as if in the war zone, and these reactions had become reflexes that they were unable to control" (Hoge, 2010, p. 52). Mike had always been able to control his reactions. His Marine infantry officer training had remained part of his core personality. The concept that my husband could not control his reactions intrigued me. Hoge also issues a challenge to readers when he adds, "To understand the experience of these warriors, the most important thing to realize is that their reactions were products of their combat survival skills—protective reflexes that were not well controlled after coming home" (2010, p. 53). Warriors return home with their combat skills intact. The plane ride across the ocean doesn't allow needed time for warriors to reset their combat survival skills before arriving home.

I was astonished by the simplicity of that statement. I had never put all of that together. Mike was able to return to us because of his combat survival skills. Without those, we would never have welcomed him home. I was humbled by this simple concept—Mike was home because he had been hyperalert, focused on the tiniest details, reacted and then thought, and all of the other combat traits that had kept him alive. Mike was "stuck" in those combat survival skills and that was a reason to be proud of him.

Hoge wrote his book for warriors to understand their reactions and how their reactions are perceived by others when they return. I read the book, however, as a guidebook to the apparent chaos in my husband's mind and spirit. Hoge explains that warriors continue to utilize all combat survival skills once they return home—they have high situational awareness, scan for threats, monitor escape routes, control emotions, and focus thought processes on survival for the warrior and for others.

> This can result in the warrior experiencing difficulty tolerating someone moving their things unexpectedly, or

> difficulty with loved ones, friends, coworkers, or anyone not following through with what they say they're going to do. When the warrior gets stressed, which is common in daily life, his body can suddenly feel like it's back in the war zone. (Hoge, 2010, p. 60)

Hoge was describing my home, but he also was providing information that I had not read before.

PTSD is full of contradictions because "virtually every reaction that mental health professionals label a 'symptom,' and which indeed can cause havoc in your life after returning home from combat, is an essential survival skill in the war zone" (Hoge, 2010, p. xii). Society desires for warriors to "dial down" when they return from combat and adapt to what society defines as a "normal" life. The skills, however, were critical for survival in combat and are difficult for warriors to dial down.

> Those who have worked in a war zone understand that their warrior responses—including responses doctors may label "PTSD"—could be needed again in the future—for instance, if they mobilize for another deployment, someone tries to break into their home, or they take a job in a dangerous profession (e.g., law enforcement, security, emergency services). *Once a warrior—always a warrior.* (Hoge, 2010, p. xii)

When warriors return from the combat zone, they still maintain their high levels of control which include the warrior constantly utilizing

> high situational awareness, scanning for threats, monitoring escape routes, controlling emotions, and keeping thought processes focused on survival, both for himself and others. This can result in the warrior experiencing difficulty tolerating someone moving

their things unexpectedly, or difficulty with loved ones, friends, coworkers, or anyone not following through with what they say they're going to do. When the warrior gets stressed, which is common in daily life, his body can suddenly feel like it's back in the war zone. (Hoge, 2010, p. 60)

The idea that moving an object could cause enough disruption that Mike could feel like he was back in the combat zone startled me. I had been fighting that level of control that he was exerting because he never had been so controlling before. I didn't realize what was happening in his decision making process (or his automatic responses) that was causing the control. We both had always been irritated by people who didn't follow through— it was one of the prime lessons we taught our kids—but Mike had gone overboard with people not following through. After reading this section, I rethought my conclusions. People who don't follow through in the combat zone can cause the death of other people. I realized that Mike had a completely different operating base than he had had before leaving for Afghanistan.

The fight-or-flight reflex had become a way of life in our household. We seemed to fight often and Mike would, when it escalated enough, walk out or threaten to move out. I was often shocked by how quickly he would want to leave. The fighting and the leaving had never been part of our marriage before. Early in our marriage, we had agreed never to allow leaving or divorcing to be an option when we disagreed. We opted out of using that; yet, I heard it so often. I was frustrated and overwhelmed at how rapidly Mike went to "I'm leaving." When I read the fight-or-flight material, I began to understand that Mike's brain was reset so that the fight-or-flight part of his brain was dominant. In this state, "rational thought and reason get compromised" (Hoge, 2010, p. 57). Sleep deprivation intensifies these reactions. I knew that Mike wasn't sleeping enough and wasn't sleeping deeply because of the nightmares. Hoge addresses the behaviors that come from sleep deprivation:

> Studies have shown that sleep deprivation significantly increases levels of anger, impulsivity, and aggression, as well as quicker and more forceful reactions to any provocation. The ability to be self-reflective and consider options is decreased, which causes decision-making to be impaired. There is increased risk-taking, decreased empathy, and decreased consideration of the long-term consequences of actions. There are also important misperceptions of thinking, termed *cognitive distortions,* which result in perceiving things as more threatening than they really are. (Hoge, 2010, p. 57)

I began to understand why, when I asked a question or took a different side, Mike thought I was attacking him. He saw me as more threatening than I meant to be and his self-reflective abilities had decreased in the three years he had spent in up-tempo mode.

"The problem for combat veterans is that the medial prefrontal cortex, the part of the brain that helps to balance out the protective reflexes, may not work well when there is sleep deprivation, high-intensity combat, or other very stressful experience" (Hoge, 2010, p. 56) I was shocked to find out that Mike really couldn't help his reactions. They were caused by the intensity of his traumatic experiences in the combat zone. "This means less control of the limbic system, which means you're more likely to overreact with anger or other fight-or-flight responses to situations that aren't particularly dangerous" (Hoge, 2010, p. 56). "Overreaction" was the best description of how I interpreted many of Mike's reactions. I had not understood how he had become so paranoid.

Hoge's explanation of anger's role in the combat zone touched me deeply. I thought of the 112 memorial services that Mike had conducted or attended, the number of wounded he had prayed with, the number of dead he had prayed over…and I was deeply moved. His anger and intensity had an explanation that was highly logical. I began to understand that he wasn't capable of friendship with me or holding hands and enjoying a fall afternoon. He was locked in the combat zone every time he closed his eyes and when he woke, he felt the remnants of the combat zone that the dawn could not erase. I felt a deep compassion for my husband as I let the following sink in:

> Emotional control, through numbing or detachment, is necessary under extreme stress. In combat, a warrior learns to turn off emotions other than anger. Anger/rage is the "fight" part of the fight-or-flight reflex, which helps the warrior neutralize the enemy. Anger masks other emotions, such as fear or sadness, allowing the warrior to do what needs to be done under fire. Even if a unit loses a team member, right after the casualty is removed or the memorial service is finished, the grief has to be put on hold when the unit goes back "outside the wire." The warrior learns to control anger itself through training, so that anger doesn't completely take over and impair the mission. Buddies help with this, and seasoned combat warriors learn how to monitor each other. After coming out of the combat environment, it can take a long time before a warrior can express a full range of emotions again. (Hoge, 2010, pp. 58-59)

I began to understand that the anger and numbness was not about me at all. I understood the logical explanation of *how* spending three years in an up-tempo combat environment can wound the spirit of a warrior. I began to see my husband differently. In the following chapter, I will explain how my changing prayers led to my spirit finding respite so that my husband could find his way back from the combat zone toward healing of his mind, body, and spirit.

This final quote from Hoge explains the scenario that most spouses of warriors with PTSD can relate to. I found it humorous when I first read it, but I also found that it bore such deep truth. Hoge describes how warriors forego patience when dealing with stupid stuff that people do in the following:

> Patience is a crucial skill in combat. You may have to wait out the enemy for days, weeks, or months before you strike, and it's not that different back home. However, many warriors completely forget this skill when they come home. They can't tolerate the stupid stuff people do, and instead of remembering to practice this skill (for example, in the supermarket line), they explode at relatively minor things. (Hoge, 2010, p. 100)

The following chart, Table 1, relates many of the combat skills that warriors learn. The first items in the table are warrior reactions in the combat zone. The second column lists some of the necessary reasons why warriors develop these skills in the combat zone. The third column explains some of the behaviors at home that the combat skills and reactions produce. The final column lists possible thoughts of the warriors who are performing these behaviors when they come home. These concepts, behaviors, and warriors' thoughts are what I gleaned from Hoge's book, *Once a Warrior Always a Warrior.*

Table 1: Combat Skills and Response in Combat Zone and at Home

Combat Skills and Responses	Purpose of Skill or Response	Warrior's Actions at Home	Warrior's Intentions
Physiological responses to danger or threat	Body responds before mind registers the danger or threat; automatic responses	Overly sensitive to possible threats and danger	Automatic responses; no intention or thought

Combat Skills and Responses	Purpose of Skill or Response	Warrior's Actions at Home	Warrior's Intentions
Physiological responses include: heightened alertness, increased mental attention, tensing muscles, higher anxiety, increased heart rate, increased blood pressure, release of adrenaline, rapid and shallow breathing	Signals imminent danger or threat; automatic response	Tense, on edge, irritable	To stay alert for danger or threats
Brain changes in the combat zone	Brain adapts its functions in order to respond to danger or threats more efficiently	Interprets many benign happenings as threats or danger	Dangers and threats are everywhere but no one is aware of them
Limbic system becomes dominant (part of brain that sets off body alarm when high threat exists)	Center of "fight-or-flight" allows rapid assessment of threat so that the chances of survival are increased; automatic change	Interprets many events as threats and responds with a fight/argument or by leaving	Survival is utmost. If can't fight, then leave
Limbic system (fight-or-flight) hijacks entire attention and entire focus	Ensures that warrior can react fast enough to survive; warriors have NO CONTROL over this hijacking	Fights over little items; threatens to or actually leaves often	No thought; just reacts
Medial pre-frontal cortex becomes less dominant; loses control of limbic system	Rational part of brain becomes secondary to the fight-or-flight part of brain; control of emotions and thought is secondary to instinctual reactions of fight-or-flight	Unable to accept rational explanations of situations; frustration	No thought; just responds as did the entire time in the combat zone

Combat Skills and Responses	Purpose of Skill or Response	Warrior's Actions at Home	Warrior's Intentions
Self-protection becomes dominant focus for warrior	Becomes primary focus of brain through physiological reactions	Warrior seems self-centered	Unaware that self focus has overtaken family focus
Sleep Deprivation	Learns to function with 4 hours of sleep; often interrupted due to night operations and attacks	Irritability, exhaustion, difficulty focusing	Exhaustion and haunted by dreams
Intense Cognitive Focus	Finely tuned thought, memory, attention, concentration; block other issues	Seems distant, can't pay attention well	Feels confused and frustrated with inability to think
Situational Awareness causes physiological reactions listed above	Constantly scanning environment for possible threats or danger; hyper-alert for threats or danger	Appears disinterested in conversation because of scanning	The scanning for danger is protection of family/friends
Ensure escape routes	Know which way to respond to danger or threat; no thought necessary when danger occurs	Have to have "just the right table" or "just the right seat" or will leave	Protecting self and family from dangers and threats
Become hyper-vigilant	Notice everything about everything in order to avoid danger or threat; constant danger requires intense vigilances	Overreaction to people approaching, backpacks, etc.	Exhaustion from constantly alert; focus on surviving
Intense Focus	Drives warriors' concentration and intensity; provides "edge" needed to survive	Focus often is on whatever is threat/danger instead of on person talking	Automatic response to intensely focus on all aspects of environment

Combat Skills and Responses	Purpose of Skill or Response	Warrior's Actions at Home	Warrior's Intentions
Scanning, tunnel vision, hypervigilance	Continually aware of environment to locate dangers and threats	Looking over and around; no focusing on speaker	Automatic response for locating threats/ danger early
Control	Control everything— emotions, reactions, etc.	Overly controlling of all details— minor and major—in family	Has to ensure family's safety
Place items EXACTLY in the right place	"Grab and go" allows warriors to grab gear for rapid use	Overreacting to items in path of exit, items left out, etc.	Items have to be in exact place for rapid response if attacked
Perform actions EXACTLY the same	Know who is doing what so they can work together	Impatient with slow actions, irritable with kids who perform tasks incorrectly	Functioning in the correct manner ensures survival for whole team
Reflexive Actions	Automatic actions; training produces reflexive actions	Reacts as if in combat zone; rapid responses can be inappropriate	No thought; just responding to training
Correct sequence of events under fire	Survival because everything works	Anger because correct sequence of events—as warrior interprets them—is not followed	Correct sequence of events has to occur for survival
Reaction Times	Shortened time between stressful event/response	Overreaction to any event	No interpretation. Automatic response
Coordination of teams	Rely on each member to respond quickly	Anger at anyone who responds slowly	Coordination is essential to teams' survival
Driving	Driving occurs in a high speed bumper to bumper setup to avoid attacks, IEDs, and other dangers or threats	High speed driving directly on bumper of car in front, weaving in and out of cars with little space	Driving habits make for a difficult target to hit

Combat Skills and Responses	Purpose of Skill or Response	Warrior's Actions at Home	Warrior's Intentions
Limited Emotions	Limited emotional responses so that emotions won't prevent focus on mission	Numb, detached, angry	Emotions will overwhelm me if I open up
Numbing	Prevent emotions from distracting from mission	Numb, detached	Doesn't have to feel all the pain and chaos if numb emotions
Detachment	Detach emotions to prevent interference with mission	Detached, disinterested in family's activities	Distancing emotions keeps warrior in control of emotions
Managing Fear and Sadness	Masked by anger; fear can be dialed up or down	Anger, intensity	Fear and sadness appear as anger because of military training
Managing Grief	Felt momentarily; put on hold until not in combat zone any long	Anger, intensity	Grief, if released, will overwhelm warrior
Managing Anger	Dominant emotion of up-tempo environment	Anger, intensity	No thought, just responding to emotional situations based on military training
Managing Anxiety	Anger overrides anxiety so that warriors can complete mission	Anger, intensity	Confused by reaction of others, normal response for warrior
Respect	Highly valued; following orders results in survival	No patience with disrespect	Respect for warriors is mandatory to ensure survival
Stupidity	Stupidity gets people killed; avoided in combat zones	Incredible impatience with people who do stupid things by warrior's interpretation	There's no excuse for stupidity. None. People die when others are stupid.

CHAPTER SEVEN

"And Bid Its Angry Tumult Cease"

Anger is a natural emotion for all humans. It is a feeling that comes and then goes rather quickly. We become angry when a driver cuts us off or someone breaks in line in front of us or our boss won't listen to our ideas. When we nurse the anger and hold onto it, we can then enter the arenas of rage, fury, hostility, resentment, or hatred. A natural emotional reaction, anger becomes a problem for warriors when warriors allow the anger to "fester or progress to persistent rage, fury, hostility, resentment, or hatred; in other words, when the immediate feeling of anger leads to a persistently angry state and behaviors and actions that have negative consequences" (Hoge, 2010, p. 156). In this chapter, we focus on how I learned new skills that created a safe environment in our home. This safe environment began to bid its (PTSD's) angry tumult to cease.

Warriors in the combat zone find anger to be an important survival skill. Their brains "reset" to respond primarily to the limbic area (the fight-or-flight area that has fear and anger as the major emotions). The more rational area of the brain that controls both emotions and the fight-or-flight response becomes secondary. Thus, warriors returning from the combat zone experience the extremes of emotions, including anger. Once home, warriors often find themselves in awkward positions. "Anger has been an important survival emotion, and there may be deep and intense feelings of anger related to things that happened during combat" (Hoge, 2010, p. 156). Warriors need a way to express their anger; however, civilians and families at home "take any expression of anger as a sign that there's a much bigger problem, a smoldering cauldron of rage waiting to pour forth" (Hoge, 2010, p. 156). As a society, we interpret anger as negative, which can lead to uninformed psychoanalysis of warriors without understanding the complexities of the emotion.

During their time in the combat zone, warriors stuffed so much anger, grief, sadness, and other emotions inside of themselves that they now fear expressing any emotion—especially anger. They fear the emotions will rapidly get out of control. As a result, legitimate feelings of anger are often stuffed inside warriors to join the other emotions clamoring to be expressed (Hoge, 2010, p. 157). Mike adds that many warriors fear the intensity of their anger in their home settings. Just as a governor on a car controls the speed limit, we have a governor (of sorts) that controls our emotions. Warriors with PTSD no longer have any governor on their emotions. They move from calm (0 mph) to explosive expression (120 mph) in milliseconds. The anger that served them well in the combat zone is now the center of many of the social irregularities.

When warriors don't express these feelings of anger or in some way acknowledge that the anger exists,

> It's more likely to fester....If the warrior doesn't find a healthy way to acknowledge and express legitimate feelings of anger, then the deep anger that may be present upon return from deployment can rapidly become a permanent condition of rage and hostility. When this happens, situations that might otherwise trigger a brief verbal expression of anger instead end up in extreme hostility, passive-aggressive behavior, confrontations, and actions that cause problems (Hoge, 2010, p. 157).

Finding healthy ways to acknowledge and express emotions can be a difficult challenge for warriors. So much chaos and pain, such deep confusion and fear—how can anyone be expected to express that much emotion in a socially acceptable manner?

Adjusting to Home

Mike had been home from Iraq for three years. We had moved twice: from NC to RI and from Newport, RI, to Columbia, SC. I had presented three or four new chaplain spouse workshops a year. I believed what I said, but recalling the good times wore me out. Each presentation required remembering who we had been and how easily we had recovered from so many deployments. The difficulties we were experiencing now frustrated me. Our earlier post-deployment adjustment behaviors and re-engagement activities were ineffective now. We had nine years of deployment in our twenty-three years married in the military. We knew deployment… or we thought we did. "Warriors and their family members are often surprised at how difficult the transition period is after coming back from a combat deployment. Many expect that they'll just need a little time for things to go back to 'normal,' but find that 'normal' is elusive and time is relative" (Hoge, 2010, p. xviii).

My rheumatoid arthritis diagnosis was joined by a fibromyalgia diagnosis. Getting out of bed was a challenge. I spent an hour or more each morning trying to get rid of my stiffness. I had to drag one or the other of my legs at times because they were not fully functioning. I often was unable to use my hands for regular tasks. My hands were usually so swollen that I could not funnel strength to them to open jars or other challenges. I worked teaching four classes a semester. Pain and fatigue were my constant companions. Mike would grow so irritated with me, acting as though I chose to be stiff, slow, or fatigued. He would encourage me to "speed up" or "keep up" when I didn't move rapidly enough. I grew more and more discouraged with the awareness that my rheumatoid arthritis had changed me so much that Mike couldn't accept who I now was. I had flare-ups of rheumatoid arthritis every three to four months over these five years.

Then there was the anger that often filled our home, though Mike kept insisting that he wasn't angry. I realize now (after asking him) that what I understood as "anger," he viewed as "intensity." What had been perfectly acceptable communication styles in the combat zone had me claiming he was "angry" at home. Mike's intensity appeared to be anger to me. I had no other interpretation for it. During this time, we had calm moments, but I had learned not to trust them. I was numbed emotionally, but the few times I felt something, it usually came out as anger. I became much less tolerant of stupidity and much less patient with pointless work. I took high doses of prednisone to try to control my disease. I looked at my hands and envisioned my joints being eaten away under the inflammation. I watched the mirror as I grew larger and larger on the medication. Moving was difficult. Feeling was difficult. Hoping was a pointless activity. I had not made any friends since we had arrived in Columbia. I controlled my emotions so tightly that I feared dumping all of it on someone else. The rheumatoid arthritis flare-ups that I had every three or four months robbed me of any energy that would allow me to be a friend.

I also had the need to protect confidentiality that affected my ability to make friends. A major rule in my parents' house was not to talk about what we heard inside of the house. As a doctor, my Dad would talk on the phone or people would drop by the house. We were taught from a young age to never mention anything we overheard because it could affect my Dad's reputation and practice. Then I married a chaplain and had the same rules for confidentiality. When Mike became a Commanding Officer, confidentiality was one lesson from the Prospective CO Spouse Course that I attended. If I had friends, I could not confide in them. If I confided any PTSD issues, then I would break Mike's trust. He trusted me to safeguard information so that he could minister effectively. In this case, so he could command effectively. Talking to anyone would mean that I was disloyal to my husband, to the Navy, and to a wounded warrior. How could I turn my back on all of that? I may have found a counselor to talk to if I had not been so very tired.

My prayers were equally numbed. I could only pray, "What should I do?" or "God, please change Mike," but I received no answers. Every now and then, I would throw in, "How can I stop this insanity?" but God did not provide an answer to that prayer either. I tried to provide an upbeat household for my two younger children who were in high school. No matter how tired or stiff I was, I went to all of their games. Mike went to the football games with me, but rarely to any other games. I tried to spin a positive explanation to the kids, but I really thought that he just didn't care to be part of the family. I tried everything I could think of to provide some relief for Mike, but he rejected all of my help. This rejection and my frustration often ended in an argument, though I was growing tired of those since nothing changed. I was so very tired and my heart was so broken. I felt helpless to provide any relief for him.

In our fourth year after Mike's return from Iraq, I began to pray for a respite from the chaos. I prayed for a respite for *me* as well as Mike. I never thought that what was going on in our home was my own "war" as some articles suggest. Those articles equate our homes as "battle zones" that are equal to what our husband experienced in Iraq and Afghanistan. We were living with the aftermath of war, but it was *not* war. (We marginalize warriors' experiences when we, as spouses, fail to understand the distinction between our home experiences and the combat experience of our spouses.) However, I was powerless to render any change in our home life. "Wives of traumatized veterans are one of various groups of persons who have been identified as suffering psychological consequences of traumatic events which they did not experience at first hand, but through their close proximity to a direct victim" (Dekel & Solomon, 2007, p. 137). I knew that I was suffering psychological consequences from interactions in my home. I just had no idea what to do about it. As a young adult, I had experienced trauma from which I learned that the world is not safe or good. At that time, I made a commitment that if I ever had kids, my home would never be a place that caused trauma to my children. Mike had supported me in that commitment when we married. The emotional intensity of our household now, however, was not a fulfillment of that promise. A wife learns, just as her husband did, "that the world is unsafe and chaotic and that being a good person does not protect one from harm. Her basic assumptions about the relationship are also upset" (Dekel & Solomon, 2007, p. 149). My world was becoming more and more chaotic, which affected me psychologically and physically. High stress triggers rheumatoid arthritis flare-ups and I had no idea how to lower the stress in my household.

In a study of 332 peacekeepers' parents, Rachel Dekel and Zahava Solomon found no evidence of secondary traumatization. Whether or not their child had PTSD, the parent groups exhibited no difference between each other. "These findings suggest that it is the intimate nature of the marital relationship that makes the wife more vulnerable to secondary traumatization than members of the extended family" (Dekel & Solomon, 2007, p. 140). Dekel and Solomon discuss a study of nine Israeli wives whose husbands have PTSD. They addressed two questions: "Why women who remain married to PTSD veterans stick it out, despite their great distress and the problems in their relationships. The other is what enables them to stay in their troubled marriages" (2007, p. 142).

The findings of this study revealed that most of the women in the study said they had considered divorce, but had decided not to go through with it. They explained "they were stopped by a strong sense of moral commitment, stemming mainly from personal loyalty and internalized social norms, but, in some cases, also from fear for their husbands' lives" (Dekel & Solomon, 2007, p. 142). These women had had good marriage relationships before their husbands developed PTSD. They described their husbands as "healthy, strong, and supportive. This, they said, reinforced their commitment to their husbands and their moral obligation to weather the difficult times with them. Their general sense was that one does not dump a man in time of hardship" (Dekel & Solomon, 2007, p. 142). One woman described her commitment as follows: "For me it's like abandoning an injured soldier on the battlefield or abandoning someone sick….We created a family together; our relationship was established before; it's not like I'd break up the whole package because he's not pulling his weight. It doesn't work like that" (Dekel & Solomon, 2007, p. 142).

In answering how they coped with the difficulties arising from PTSD, the women shared several reasons, including:

- The good feelings they had from earlier times in their marriage

- Their appreciation of their husband's courage and determination as he struggled each day

- His example inspired them to continue their struggle as well

- Their love for their husband

- The sense of strength and empowerment they gained from their own struggle to help their husbands and keep the family together. (Dekel & Solomon, 2007, pp. 142-143).

For me, divorce was not an option. No matter how numb, fatigued, or alone I was, I was NOT going to walk out on my husband. I had committed to him for life in a vow before God. I had committed to be with him through his military career. I had committed to minister with him to military families. I couldn't justify quitting because times were hard. Mike had always supported me through difficult times. How could I just walk out on him? Leaving was not an option; but changing didn't seem to be an option either.

We had been attending a church that Mike insisted that we attend even though none of us were able to worship there. One of my doctors recommended a church downtown that we visited one Sunday. Sitting in a church that was filled with the Holy Spirit was such a relief for my spirit, mind, and body. We all felt the Holy Spirit's presence and we began going to that church. I felt such a comfort by just attending the services at the church. I did not know, however, how I would journey deeper into God's way than I had ever known I could. For that period of time, I began receiving enough spiritual strength to go through the week from Sunday to Sunday.

Changing Bit by Bit

Slowly, as I read and re-read *Once a Warrior Always a Warrior*, I began to comprehend that I didn't understand anything about Mike anymore. I realized that my interpretations of his behaviors were so far off track. I was relating to Mike as though he was the same man who pinned on his eagles and boarded the plane for Afghanistan. His actions and his motives were clear to me or I thought they were; however, I was using the wrong lens to view his actions, motives, and thoughts. I pondered this new information for awhile.

I reread parts of the book. The possibility that I had spent all of these years—four since he had returned from Iraq—totally misunderstanding Mike and his motivations was overwhelming. One evening after dinner, I went into Mike's study. I had the book with me.

"Can I ask you something?"

"What?" he said, with his usual irritation at being interrupted.

"In this book, there is a story about a guy who sat down in a medical office and found at least two exits, looked for anything threatening, chose a seat where he could see everyone, and then left because a little girl had a backpack that he couldn't see inside.

He didn't know if it had explosives or other weapons inside. He had been home from Vietnam about 30 years when he did that."

By this time, Mike had turned in his chair and faced me. I asked, "Do you do that when you enter places?"

"Yes, all the time."

"Everywhere you go?"

"Yes. It's called 'threat assessment.' I do it everywhere all the time."

I stared at him for a minute and Mike grew uncomfortable. "Is that all?" he asked.

I left the study. I thought of all of the places where we had been and how I never knew that he was doing a threat assessment. I just thought he was being a difficult customer or an irritable person. Why hadn't he told me this? Why did he need to do it?

I spent a lot of time thinking and rereading parts of the book over the next few days. I began to see that safety was a huge issue for warriors in the combat zone. Even though it should be obvious, I just never was aware that it lasted so long. We live in a small town where little to nothing happens. Why do threat assessments?

A few evenings later, I asked Mike, "Do you feel safe in our home?"

He responded rapidly, "No."

I said "really" and then "why not" which were not the best conversation starters. He replied, "I just don't" and walked out of the room.

As I stood there, a huge wave of compassion flowed over me. My heart broke for my husband. Everything that I had thought I knew about him and everything I had decided were his motives was wrong. I had barricaded my emotions away to keep from getting hurt when he was feeling our home was not a place of safety. I had become numb near the beginning of the Iraq deployment and had not found a way to move out of the numbness. But this wave of compassion awoke what had been buried inside me.

In that moment, I felt the hand of God on me. Warmth rushed through me as I saw my husband as a broken man, trying his best to hold on. I saw the incredible energy he was using to protect himself and to try to keep control of the chaos that threatened to engulf him. In that instant, my prayers changed from "Fix Mike" to "Who should I be to ease Mike's pain? How can I respond to his wound?"

The compassion that I felt led me from holding firm boundaries and using a confrontational accountability to more of a relational accountability with flexible boundaries. I held myself accountable to the commitment that I had made years ago. I found strength inside me that I knew I did not have. In hindsight, I am aware that what I experienced was the Holy Spirit empowering me and guiding me. I still felt the effects of rheumatoid arthritis, the flare-ups, the pain, and the fatigue, but I felt strength in my spirit that allowed me to begin to formulate a plan to reach Mike. I went to our new church physically, emotionally, and spiritually drained. Each Sunday I received enough strength to take me to the next Sunday. I slowly learned a deeper and deeper trust in God. Robert Grant explains this experience as follows: "Human care, in conjunction with divine assistance," enables people to set aside their own egos and desires so that they can become strong enough to "allow the deeper dimensions of [their spirits] to emerge" (1996, p. 13). The Holy Spirit empowered me to be able to find ways to reach Mike. I began to live from deeper dimensions of my life through the help of the Holy Spirit.

For the next few weeks, I asked Mike questions. I found out that we sat in a certain place in church because it was strategically the best place to reach exits if we needed to. We never moved to the middle of the pew—even when asked—because we could not exit rapidly. I understood that the reason the kids' shoes and belongings had to be out of the way had to do with exiting rapidly when needed. This necessity was a survival skill.

I began to understand that much of what I had interpreted as "against me" had little or nothing to do with me. For example, my limited, slow movements and Mike's impatience with me— Mike had switched into survival mode, reacting to the danger that my slow movements placed us in. He had not thought through anything. He had just reacted to the situation that I was creating.

His ultimate goal was to ensure my safety, which couldn't be achieved when I walked so slowly. His reactions did not mean that he couldn't understand or accept my limitations. He wasn't focused on me at all. Microsecond delays get people killed in the combat zone. His reactions meant that he was responding to a higher priority, a priority that gave us a better chance of survival. What I had interpreted as rejection was actually a tremendous expression of love.

I learned how angry I made Mike when I ignored or argued with his attempts to keep our family safe. I thought he was just overly controlling with details. I didn't realize that he was working from survival mode and desiring to protect all of us. As I look back, I can understand some of his anger with me because I was not at all anywhere near survival mode in my plans and decisions.

I began to understand that he was unable to attend our daughter's basketball game because the "boom, boom" of stomping feet on the bleachers caused his physiological reactions to begin and took him back to the combat zone. The gym was in a pit at the school with difficult escape routes. To Mike, the whole place was a death trap. I also learned that the kids had to perform tasks exactly as Mike wanted because tasks that are performed poorly get people killed.

I understood Mike's inability to tolerate stupid people and incompetence. Part of his problem with attending some of the kids' games had to do with stupid coaches. Instead of losing control and embarrassing the kids, he just didn't attend. Mike's demand for order and exactness was something that kept him alive in the combat zones. I began to appreciate the efforts that he had gone to in order to stay alive. Most of all, I began to understand that most of this had little or nothing to do with me. When Mike became so intense, his mind and body were *reacting* to threats and danger. I just happened to be the recipient of his intensity because I was there. Often, the intensity wasn't even directed at me. It was just the *automatic response* that Mike had developed over the duration of three years in the combat zone.

I stopped being embarrassed because he would ask a waitress to seat us somewhere else. There were many behaviors that I started accepting and stopped feeling embarrassed over—behaviors that didn't fit the proper rules of society. I decided that before anyone could judge Mike's actions, they needed to spend as much time as Mike had in the combat zone.

My understanding of his actual motives and his reasons for his actions grew and grew. Mike and I began to discuss his reactions. I would ask him about different incidents and he was able to tell me what was going on with him. I learned why we had to leave our son's graduation so rapidly. He explained the importance of exactness and of so many different behaviors. I was so overwhelmed to realize that the whole graduation incident had to do with his love and protection of our family.

My heart, which I had numbed and hardened, was broken. I had committed to a life in the Navy and I had committed to support my husband; yet, when he needed me most, I had not been there for him. I felt bad for a day or so and then I decided that I would change that. I would figure out how to relieve him of some of the reactions from combat. My goal was to give him a respite from the war…no matter how small.

After prayer, I decided that I could remove some of his fear by making our home safe. I was guessing about the fear based on Hoge's statements that follow:

> Fear actually can become much more of a problem for a warrior after coming home than it is in the war zone. The fear signal, which becomes almost a sixth sense in the combat environment, and which the warrior learns to trust implicitly for survival, can remain on high alert back home where there is no longer the same need for it. At home, "locking and loading" is not going to be useful very often, and the warrior can find himself in frustrating situations where he has no outlet for channeling the fear signal going off in his brain and body.

Sharply honed combat skills that helped the warrior control fear in combat may prove counterproductive on the home front, and result in the warrior not knowing what to do when the fear alarm sounds. (2010, pp. 25-26)

Over the next few months, I focused on several areas in our home that might allow Mike a respite from the war. From these trials, I learned three lessons that include:

- Being safe at home

- Bringing order and structure to our home

- Making accommodations for Mike's wound.

Through these lessons that I learned, my prayer "to bid its angry tumult cease" began to be answered.

Lesson 1: Safe at Home

From the time my first child was born, my goal was to make my home a safe place for my family. My kids weren't allowed to be mean to each other or make fun of each other because I wanted them to feel that they were safe at home. Knowing that my husband had spent four years not feeling safe was overwhelming. But I prayed and asked God to give me the actions to take so that Mike could feel safe again.

In *The Wounded Healer*, Henri Nouwen answers the question of "How does healing take place?" with the answer, "hospitality" (1972, pp. 88-89). Initially, I stumbled through attempts to establish a safe home. As I opened myself more and more to God's guidance, I became more successful. I discovered Nouwen's reading awhile after creating a safe home for Mike. Several years later, I found that what the Holy Spirit planted in my spirit was echoed in Nouwen's writings. I learned to respond to the Spirit's leading without questioning. Nouwen writes,

> Hospitality is the virtue which allows us to break through the narrowness of our own fears and to open our houses to the stranger, with the intuition that salvation comes to us in the form of a tired traveler. Hospitality makes anxious disciples into powerful witnesses, makes suspicious owners into generous givers, and makes close-minded sectarians into interested recipients of new ideas and insights. (1972, p. 89)

Opening my door to a stranger was what I had done when Mike returned. As I left behind my game of thinking that deployments and three years spent primarily in the combat zone affected Mike the same way, I began to view him as a stranger who was welcome in my home.

Step 1: Word Choice My first step was to stop arguing with Mike, even when I disagreed. Before I responded, I would ask myself, "Is this something that I would argue with a guest about?" If the answer was "no," then I kept my response to myself. Keeping my mouth shut was incredibly difficult. Not responding created great stress within me (which lead to a flare-up or two), but I gradually learned to obey the Spirit's guidance and hold my tongue. It took awhile but I mastered it.

I also began to be aware of how I spoke to Mike—my tone and my word choice. I spoke to him as I would to a guest in my home, which meant I was much more pleasant than I had been. Mike responded in very small, positive ways so I was encouraged.

Nouwen presents hospitality as a healing power. I was familiar with hospitality as a gift of the Holy Spirit (not mine though), but was intrigued with "hospitality as a healing power." Nouwen first defines hospitality as "the ability to pay attention to the guest. This is very difficult, since we are preoccupied with our own needs, worries and tensions, which prevent us from taking distance from ourselves in order to pay attention to others" (1972, p. 89). I prayed daily that God would help me focus on Mike's needs and not on my own. I slowly began to develop trust in Mike again. I stopped feeling that I had to defend myself and, instead, paid attention to my "guest."

I stopped arguing and just bit my tongue. I realized that when I argued, I became a threat to Mike. He responded to the threat as he responded to threats in the combat zone. My arguing was triggering his survival instincts; thus, I unknowingly exacerbated his PTSD. I noticed that Mike wasn't exploding as much and he wasn't going from zero to off the scale with his reactions. It was extremely difficult to keep my mouth shut, but I felt my spirit slowly healing as I did. When my focus was on my "guest," *my* spirit began to heal. I began—very slowly—to be less numb. With the loss of the numbness, I began to feel the presence of the Holy Spirit in my life again. I began to feel that my spirit was slowly healing after a long illness. Nouwen notes that if a person wants to truly pay attention to another person (without placing his own intentions or needs above that person's), then he "has to be at home in his own house—that is, he has to discover the center of his life in his own heart." In approaching Mike by extending hospitality to a guest, I was able to return to feeling at home in my own house. I rediscovered the center of my life in my own heart. With that, I was able to again respond to the Holy Spirit.

Step 2: Slowing Down Mike's attempted control over me bothered me deeply. Even though I understood the importance of control in the combat zone, I struggled to breathe some days. I prayed about what I should do. The answer I received parallels Nouwen's writings:

> When our souls are restless, when we are driven by thousands of different and often conflicting stimuli, when we are always 'over there' between people, ideas and the worries of this world, how can we possibly create the room

and space where someone else can enter freely without feeling himself an unlawful intruder? (1972, p. 90)

My prayer was to find a way to bring relief to Mike; yet, I wanted to be able to continue to be driven by thousands of conflicting stimuli. The many activities that I was involved in meant that Mike could not "enter freely" or find the room and space to heal. How could he feel safe when I could not provide an environment that was safe from threats and dangers?

I quit several activities I was doing that Mike didn't like me doing. I began to be home when Mike was home. I went to the kids' games and school events, but I focused on developing a place where Mike could feel safe. Before he could truly open up the pent up emotions that he had brought home, he had to feel confident that he had a safe environment. Each time I prayed, I was given peace that this was the direction to go. I began to notice that Mike was a bit surer of himself when I was home and open to him. I also became much more focused on being thankful to have him home from the war. As I prayed, my attitude changed from a bit (or more) of resentment to an attitude of a nurturing, healing presence for his chaotic mind. Sunday to Sunday, the Holy Spirit refreshed me.

Step 3: Safe Spaces I would have issues with what Mike had said, but I didn't argue with him. I found a way to discuss the *issue* with him. I went to him when there was little stress. This time usually was two or three days after the event occurred. I would ask Mike when the event in question happened, did he feel _____ (threatened, trapped, angry, etc.) He would think about the event, locate his feelings, and then respond with "Yes, I felt that way" or "No, I felt (another way)," but he would name his own feelings. In this way, Mike began to remember the full range of feelings. He also could analyze the situation. This analyzing moved to the point that he was able to pinpoint his feelings and state a better response than the one he had done. I created safe spaces for him to analyze his emotions, which gradually allowed him to begin expressing a full range of emotions again.

After those questions worked well, I began to ask Mike about his motivations. I would begin with, "I need to ask you about something" and follow that with "Did you mean to hurt my feelings when you interrupted me at such and such event?" Mike would always say that he did not intend to hurt my feelings. He would then describe the scenario that he was responding to. We always had two different experiences at the same event. Mike began to be more sensitive to how he treated us, slowly moving from survival mode to husband/father.

During this time, Mike slowly began to trust me more and more. That trust caused him to begin to lean on me bit by bit. After a year or so, I found that Mike was leaning on me for much of his life. I feared I would not be able to support him, but again, the Holy Spirit provided for me when I thought I had no more strength.

Lesson 2: Order and Structure

Because I now understood the reasons for escape routes to be clear, I made the kids either line their shoes up neatly out of the doorway or take them to their rooms. The exits were always free of belongings and any clutter. I made sure that Mike's clothes and other items were where they should be. I stopped expecting rationality from him because I realized that when he responded rapidly that he was responding from his limbic system (the fight-or-flight) section of his brain. He reacted without thought. His actions were automatic responses. This way of responding had become who he was as he spent over three years in the up-tempo pace.

I made extra efforts to keep Mike informed of the kids' activities. I texted him from the games that he couldn't attend with updates on how the kids and teams were doing. I found that if I explained my physical issues to Mike, then he was more accepting of them. I didn't wait until we were supposed to be somewhere to tell him. Instead, I would announce the night before if I was having a physical challenge at the time. For example, if we were going to an official function, I would ask, "What time are we leaving?" Mike would tell me and I would say, "I'm having trouble with my right leg. It's sort of stiff. My good shoes aren't going to allow me to walk fast. Do we need to leave earlier?" Then Mike was prepared for me to be slower and could adjust the time we left if needed. Thus, my physical state became part of the plan. We then executed the plan without surprises, slow downs, or contingencies.

Lesson 3: Accommodations

The actual extent of Mike's wound was the biggest revelation that I had from *Once a Warrior Always a Warrior*. As our home became safer for Mike, it became safer for the kids and me, too. As I continued to observe Mike's behavior, I found that Hoge's explanations of the warrior home from the war fit Mike. As I considered the impact of his war wound, I began to think of ways to help ease his way. He was in counseling at the time, so it was natural that I wanted to support him in that.

Step 1: Immediate Family. Family was the first step. I began to explain Mike's wound to our children. I had always been open about our moves and about what was going on with their Dad when he was deployed (war or otherwise). I told them why their Dad reacted as he did and that he wasn't in control of all of his responses. I explained the concepts of *duration* (their Dad had been in up-tempo war pace for three years), *intensity* (the demands on their Dad as far as comforting the dying, praying for the dead, etc.), and *proximity* (how their Dad had been in the middle of so much death and grieving). I also explained "automatic responses" which was more difficult for the kids to understand. How could their Dad not be in control of something? It was a harder concept, but I was clear with my explanations. I was open with them, listening to their responses. I found that with more understanding, they became very protective of their Dad. Over the next years, I continued analyzing Mike's behaviors and explaining to the kids the reasons their Dad reacted as he did (see Table 1).

Step 2: Extended Family. When extended family called and Mike didn't want to talk, I didn't put him on the phone. I always answered the phone. If family events became too loud, I encouraged Mike to go somewhere quieter. I gave Mike permission to leave when, in the past, I considered such actions as really, really bad manners. Mike didn't want to have to pretend to be happy for pictures. So I intervened on his behalf. I told family members directly that he wouldn't participate. If they said anything negative, I just ignored them or stated that war changes people. I ran interference for Mike. I didn't care if family members accepted my explanations or not. Accommodating Mike's wound was my primary mission.

Step 3: Lessen Stress. Just as we would have made accommodations if Mike came home in a wheelchair, I viewed our house and his life as areas that needed accommodations. Whatever I found highly stressed him or caused him to react rapidly, I tried to avoid the situation or prepare him for it. I found that talking through an upcoming event and discussing possible areas that would cause stress was an excellent way for Mike to handle the stress without relying on the fight-or-flight part of his brain. As the months passed, I saw more and more of the woundedness of Mike's spirit. I arranged events and happenings as much as I could so that he would enjoy them and not have to be in the awkward position of reacting before thinking. He slowly became better able to handle unexpected situations as the months passed.

Respite

When I would think of Mike's PTSD, the image in my mind had changed from a controlling, angry husband to a broken man whose wounded spirit was still hobbling through the combat zone. I realized that I was doing far less than the families whose warriors had massive physical wounds. I felt deeply grateful that Mike had returned to us. I realized the cost of his surviving three years in the combat zone was his inability to return fully. Sunday to Sunday, the Holy Spirit changed my heart.

Over the next year, I found myself actually worshipping in church again. I began to find a deep peace that lasted through the service, at least. It was the respite for my spirit that I had prayed for. Nouwen asks, "What does hospitality as a healing power require? It requires first of all that the host feel at home in his own house, and secondly that he create a free and fearless place for the unexpected visitor" (1972, p. 89). I began to feel at home in my home and in my spirit. My physical needs still existed, but the rheumatoid arthritis had slowed me down from activities and my commitment to a safe home had slowed me down more. As I slowed down, I began to feel healing within my spirit. I felt healing and peace. "Paradoxically, by withdrawing into ourselves, not out of self-pity but out of humility, we create the space for another to be himself and to come to us on his own terms" (Nouwen, 1972, p. 91). I withdrew into myself so that I was more attuned to Mike's needs. Sunday to Sunday, the Holy Spirit healed my weary spirit.

As the months passed, I tried out the concept I read about that Mike had an identity problem. I read about identity problems as being part of PTSD. When we had moved to Columbia, Mike had insisted that we attend a kind of church that we had not attended for many years. He began men's groups and took them on hikes and such. He continued starting activities until he was exhausted. The pattern that he developed seemed to imitate his life. He returned to worshipping in a kind of church that had worked for him when he was young. Outdoor activities—shared with other men and not the family—imitated his life as a young man. Other actions imitated his younger life as well. It was as though Mike had forgotten who he was. By imitating old behaviors, it seemed that he hoped to find himself again. Mike had lost his bearings in life. As he felt safer at home, he began to loosen his grip on these re-creations of his early life. He leaned on me more and more.

We had developed a tentative communication style that grew stronger by the month. Mike would become upset about something, vocalize his objections with intensity, and then reach conclusions that I disagreed with. An example is that he would ask me a question. I would answer and he would interpret my tone as sarcastic. He then would react by showing intensity, which appeared to me as anger. I would stop responding (my safe home reaction). Then, a few days later, I would approach Mike and we would calmly discuss the event. He was able to hear my interpretations and my intentions. I was able to hear how my responses affected him. We both listened to the other one and then we changed according to what the other said. This process was very slow, but it began to draw us closer together. Mike points to this time as a time when he began to trust me again and he began to feel safe again.

As Mike's confidence began to build, he started facing the depth of his wound. None of the re-living of an earlier life or easy answers were working for him. Therapy was helping to calm him somewhat. The hospitality seemed to be offering a balm for his wounded spirit. God was working through me to touch Mike's spirit. Nouwen speaks to suffering and the start of liberation in the following:

> Perhaps the main task of the minister is to prevent people from suffering for the wrong reasons. Many people suffer because of the false supposition on which they have based their lives. That supposition is that there should be no fear or loneliness, no confusion or doubt. But these sufferings can only be dealt with creatively when they are understood as wounds integral to our human condition. Therefore ministry is a very confronting service. It does not allow people to live with illusions of immortality and wholeness. It keeps reminding

others that they are mortal and broken, but also that with the recognition of this condition, liberation starts. (Nouwen, 1972, p. 93)

I was lonely during this time; however, the differences that I saw in Mike began to encourage me. Mike was slowly moving toward facing the full extent of his wounded spirit. He was discarding depending on himself and slowly moving toward liberation from the chaos in his mind.

Unable to find complete relief in therapy, rebuilding his identity, or jobs, Mike slowly stopped all of the activities and began to face inward. Recognizing that he was not going to find the event or the activity that would take away his wound, Mike slowed down and began to rely on me. The spiritual wound, which is the core of PTSD, is what he finally began to face. At that time, I didn't realize what was occurring between us. It was not until I read about hospitality as a healing ministry in Nouwen that I began to understand the power of a safe home. Mike was able to begin to face his wound–his spirititual wound–because of the ministry of hospitality in our house. Facing this spiritual wound requires great courage and commitment. Nouwen explains this concept with:

> Why is this a healing ministry? It is healing because it takes away the false illusion that wholeness can be given by one to another. It is healing because it does not take away the loneliness and the pain of another, but invites him to recognize his loneliness on a level where it can be shared. Many people in this life suffer because they are searching for the man or woman, the event or encounter, which will take their loneliness away. But when they enter a house with real hospitality they soon see that their own wounds must be understood not as sources of despair and bitterness, but as signs that they have to travel on in obedience to the calling sounds of their own wounds. (1972, p. 92)

Across time, Mike began to share small bits of his pain and shame with me. As he did, he moved closer to the calling sounds of his wound, the sounds that were calling him to an authentic experience with God.

Calmness crept into our home in snatches and moments. As Mike opened up more and more, his dependence on me grew deeper and deeper. Slowly, he released some of the emotions he kept inside. As he released the emotions, he sorted them out, fighting some of them and embracing others. I wasn't sure that I had the strength to support Mike as much as he needed me. I prayed for strength daily. Sunday to Sunday, God strengthened me through worship.

During this time, my father moved to a care facility about twenty minutes from our home. He had been living about two hours away, but his dementia worsened and he needed more care. I visited Dad daily, spending an hour or two with him. My Dad and I had always been close so visiting him daily brought joy to me. We often walked in the garden and talked a bit. As the year went by, Dad struggled more and more to find the words that he wanted to describe something. I was able to figure out most of what he was trying to think of, and that gave him great relief.

The garden at the care facility was peaceful and I enjoyed that peace and the beauty of the flowers. I had always adored my dad, so watching his slow decline saddened me deeply; yet, I treasured the time to be able to walk with Dad from this life to the next. I taught university classes, went by to provide support for my father, and then went home to provide support to my husband. My daughter was in high school and my middle son had just started college. When I read Dekel and Solomon's writings, I chuckled at one of the quotes from the book. I didn't know there was such a concept as "compassion fatigue" that applied to spouses. I thought the concept was only for professional counselors and therapists. Dekel and Solomon's presentation of this concept means that wives sacrifice too much of themselves and too many of their own needs "in their efforts to improve their husbands' situation and to preserve their family life" (Dekel & Solomon, 2007, p. 139). I was also disturbed by this idea. I kept thinking, if not me, then who would take care of my family? Sunday to Sunday, God was with me.

While I was caring for my father, Mike became much more supportive than he had been since coming home. He recognized how difficult watching my Dad decline was for me. Even though Mike still leaned on me for support, he started supporting me when I needed it with my Dad. I began to understand deep in my spirit the healing that Mike had begun to experience through the ministry of hospitality. Once again, I found Nouwen's writings to explain what my spirit was experiencing. Mike and I were finding our way to hope.

> Through this common search, hospitality becomes community. Hospitality becomes community as it creates a unity based on the shared confession of our basic brokenness and on a shared hope. This hope in turn leads us far beyond the boundaries of human togetherness to Him who calls His people away from the land of slavery to the land of freedom. It belongs to the central insight of the Judaeo-Christian tradition, that it is the call of God which forms the people of God. (Nouwen, 1972, pp. 93-94)

The more I surrendered to the Holy Spirit's guidance, the more Mike was drawn to the Holy Spirit through my actions of hospitality. Through this process, we began slowly to form "community" again. Mike found the stability he needed to begin his arduous spiritual journey.

> *Love is not a victory march…*
> *It's a cold and it's a broken "Hallelujah."*
> *–Leonard Cohen*

CHAPTER EIGHT

"And Hushed Their Raging at Thy Word"

Shame. Guilt. Judgment. My shame grew deeper and deeper as the years passed and I was still struggling with the changes in me from my experiences in the combat zone. As a Christian, I should be able to forgive myself, as I have taught others to do so often. I distinctly remember thinking to myself, that as a chaplain, I should be able to get control of this chaos that brewed just below the surface. I kept going through motions, but nothing was working. I couldn't look at myself objectively to understand what was happening inside of me. I thought when people found out that I was diagnosed with PTSD, they would say things such as, "Look how weak he is," "His emotions are out of control," and "He can't follow his own advice." I struggled to make sense of how I came home with PTSD. I kept running my diagnosis over and over in my mind: "Moderate to Severe PTSD." I felt such extreme shame that I shut down even more than I had when I first came home. I was ashamed. I felt so weak and out of control. I felt that I had let everyone down. After all, chaplains just do not get PTSD! The shame I felt was intense, and it was coupled with the sense that I was a failure. I had come to the point where I tried to protect myself no matter the cost. I usually interpreted stressful encounters as an attack on my family or me.

I remember thinking that I was totally alone. I was completely responsible for protecting my family and myself...no matter what the consequences were.

After retiring from thirty-six years of military service, I became the new Professor of Chaplaincy at a local university and seminary. I was constantly surprised by people's summations of the military, in general, but also of me personally. The concept of "mental illness," which includes being broken and labeled as intense and angry, places such a negative stigma on warriors who have the diagnosis. People assume they understand, but unless they have been in the military and combat, they do not fully understand. They think they do, but they really do not understand at all. Their lack of understanding—and desire to understand—can cause the warrior's traumatic injury to become an even deeper injury (Grant, 1996, p. 36). Hoge's comments about returning to a three-dimensional world after experiencing a fourth dimension and trying to sort out who is crazy—me or them—came back to me (2010, p. xiv). What hurt the most, though, was that Kathy couldn't understand and I couldn't find a way to explain to her what was happening inside of me. The pain was intense; the dreams were vivid and horrifying. Experiencing a fourth dimension that differed from everything that I had previously known explains exactly how I felt. I didn't have the military, a way of life I'd know for so many years, to lean on or fall back on anymore. Now, I was retired and no longer a part of the active duty system.

In *The Way of the Wound*, Robert Grant writes:

> Trauma can shut down indefinitely several, if not all, levels of one's being, depending on age, maturity and type of trauma. These are just a few of the factors that influence the severity and intensity of the traumatic response....Unresolved trauma temporarily or permanently throws victims into a survival mode. Trauma disrupts abilities to form or maintain a self, along with

abilities to develop increasingly more mature and flexible modes of relating. (1996, p. 11)

The duration of time I spent in the combat zone (three years) along with the intense exposure to traumatic events was an initial factor as to why I came home with PTSD. The intensity of the environment—especially at Camp Fallujah, and the other locations I visited in Al Anbar Province, Iraq —added to the trauma. My proximity to so many traumatic events is the third reason that I had responded by remaining "locked and loaded" in up-tempo mode when I had returned from Iraq. Not only did I witness so much trauma, death, and brokenness, but I heard detailed, graphic story after detailed, graphic story of trauma, horror, and death experienced by the Marines, sailors, and soldiers I spoke to on a daily basis. I knew all of this, but I was unable to help myself. I knew how to help other people, but I remained numbed and in survival mode. Only I didn't stop long enough to realize that I was in survival mode. I was rapidly running out of the inner ability to go on.

Counseling

Kathy approached me one day during the summer after I retired and suggested that I might want to consider returning to therapy. I rejected the idea at first, so she just laid a note card with a VA VET Center counselor's name and phone number on the table and walked off. She had found me another counselor. This time she had run into a friend who introduced her to the wife of a counselor at the VA VET Center. That led to a phone number exchange and there was the paper with the name and number of another counselor staring at me.

In the summer that I retired, I found myself meeting with a counselor at the VA VET Center in Columbia, SC. After a few sessions, he began discussing with me the experiences that were common to individuals who were diagnosed with PTSD upon their return from the combat zone. The counselor recognized that I was in my survival mode behavior and needed intervention to build a new understanding and set of skills that would provide a better quality of life. He gave me the book, *Once a Warrior Always a Warrior*, which contained many helps that described in technical terms what was going on inside of me and why I was responding to stimuli the way I was. Hoge suggests many ways to control the automatic explosive reactions, remnants of the survival skills that were necessary in the combat zone. The up-tempo pace was so ingrained in me that I lived in that mode and reacted without thinking. It had become an automatic response to threat, danger, and stupidity. Kathy often asked why I was so angry. I would tell her that I wasn't angry. I finally found the word I needed. It wasn't anger I was expressing, it was "intensity."

I also found that my spiritual life, my relationship with God, was distant. There were times when I felt God had abandoned me, I cried out to him often, "Oh God where are you?" I wasn't sure how to break out of the barriers of protection that I had erected to protect myself. I was afraid to step outside of my self-made protective barriers. These barriers I had raised to protect me were the same barriers separating me from my family, my friends, and my God. I no longer was in contact with the warriors that I had been in the combat zone with. I talked with them some, but being retired erected a whole new set of barriers. Judith Herman explains:

> Traumatic events call into questions basic human relationships. They breach the attachments of family, friendship, love, and community. They shatter the construction of the self that is formed and sustained in relation to others. They undermine the belief systems that give meaning to human experience. They violate the victim's faith in a natural or divine order and cast the victim into a state of existential crisis. (1997, p. 51)

An "existential crisis" was exactly what I was experiencing and the words are an excellent description of how I felt. I no longer understood how to apply the meanings that had defined my prewar life. They no longer worked. I didn't trust any understanding that I had previously had. I was in an acute crisis of trying to remember who I was and to understand who I had become. My mental, physical, and spiritual interpretations of the world were in disarray.

Chaos and Confusion

I was in my fifties when I left for Afghanistan. I was not a young adult still in the discovery process of my full identity. I knew who I was. I understood my relationships with family and friends. The words, "existential crisis," in no way applied to me. My wife was my best friend and we had a great relationship. My faith was deep and had carried me through many crises. I thrived in my work. My mind, body, and spirit were unified. Yet, at this point in my life, I was unsure how to stop this pain, this chaos that filled my brain, threatening to overcome me at any time. I had stuffed so much emotion inside of me for so many years that there was no room left. Those emotions I had stuffed inside were now starting to spill out in ways that were uncontrollable and often inappropriate. Those emotions were boiling over into almost every aspect of my life. I had to maintain constant control of the emotions while trying to remember who I was. I felt alone in the midst of this existential crisis. For a time period, I felt like God was not listening to me or possibly didn't care to hear me. While I realized logically that feeling distant from God is part of an existential crisis, I found myself floundering without His presence to guide me.

I started to try ways to feel God's presence that had worked for me earlier in life. My goal was to relieve the pain and chaos that was controlling my life. I made the family join a church that the rest of the family didn't like. It reminded me of a church that I had grown up in. A place where I had come to know Jesus Christ and His love, care, and provisions. That kind of church had worked for me once, so maybe it would again. I started men's groups and took them on rope courses and other physical challenges. I really enjoyed working with men and helping them build new relational skills with God and their families. I had always found help, peace, and serenity in times of crisis through running or other physical activities. I loved to go on long runs that allowed me to get lost in my thoughts and prayers as I ran with no one bothering me. For most of the men, the physical activities that I introduced them to were new experiences for them. Most of the men had never done such activities. Within a few months, they slowly began to drop out. However, these events and others acted as a bandage on my wounds. Later, I realized I was attempting to escape my own pain by helping others. If I focused on their pain, then I could possibly forget my own pain.

For a short time, that approach worked. I felt useful as a chaplain again, but that feeling didn't last long. No matter what I tried that had worked in the past, I couldn't find any peace from the chaos in my mind and spirit. Nothing worked for me. I could not find my way back to God. I was running from the pain and chaos of the trauma as well as God and his Spirit who were calling me into the wound. I was drifting, anchorless in a storm. "Traumatic healing demands that all important aspects of a trauma be brought into the light of awareness and owned – otherwise symptoms are the result" (Grant, 1996, p. 36). Facing the deeper aspects of my traumatic wound was overwhelming.

I discovered that I was alienating my family, but I didn't know how to change. I loved them and knew that what I was doing was not healthy, but I could not stop. If I felt strong negative feelings, then they came out in explosive bursts. I worked to prevent expressing any emotions because of my intense fear of not being able to control them. So I stuffed them deeper inside, or so I thought. When the explosive bursts did erupt from within me, I felt such relief as if I was letting off steam; however, I also felt extreme guilt over the outbursts. I should not feel better from these outbursts because my calling as a chaplain did not allow me to explode with negative emotions. My role as husband and father didn't support that behavior either. Most of all, my

Christian faith didn't support it. I did my best to keep the intensity controlled but, after awhile, the intensity erupted and I had explosive outbursts. I felt great shame for this behavior, because I knew that society and the church did not condone such behavior. Occasionally, I had a less intense outburst at work. Work was one of the places where I felt as if people judged my behavior and judged it harshly. The continual experiences of attempting to control these emotional eruptions became debilitating.

"Trauma brutally awakens consciousness and disrupts cognitive, behavioral and interpersonal ways of organising reality.... Traumatic stress plays on inherent vulnerabilities and demonstrates that habitual ways of taking up reality no longer work" (Grant, 1996, p. 29). I found that every part of my consciousness became consumed by this trauma. I wanted relief, but I found that nothing I tried worked. "Trauma destroys an innocence that would prefer to be active, confident and risk-free rather than accepting that death and uncertainty are forever at hand" (Grant, 1996, p. 29). I wanted to escape the death, the smells, the sights, the fears, the dying, the horrors with which I had lived for so many years. I wanted a respite from the war, but none was to be found. After coming home from the wars, I thought I would be getting away from those horrors. But they continually appeared in my dreams and thoughts during times of work, leisure, relaxation, or any activity.

Following the desire of our traumatized self to seek safety in the old ways is a normal reaction to traumatic stress. This attempt, however, fails because trauma has taught us lessons that the old world is not safe and that we have to find meaning that incorporates the lessons from the traumatic events that we have experienced. Grant writes, "Trying to deal with the impact of their injuries causes most victims to run into the very systems that once protected them. Now on the outside and looking in, victims are shunned and feared by members of the collective" (1996, p. 35). The traumatized person wants the people around them to acknowledge the depth of their trauma; yet, people do not want to acknowledge that the world they have carefully crafted may not be safe and probably will not protect them from traumatic events. The presence of a traumatized person reminds other people that they could be the next ones to suffer trauma. In the Western world, we shun such reminders. The presence of traumatized persons become an irritation to others.

Grant continues,

> Victims demand that issues laid open by their traumatic injuries be collectively owned. Pain and horror demand that others take notice of what is being avoided. If validation is not forthcoming then victims end up feeling inadequate, crazy, isolated and doubting the validity of their own experience. Unacknowledged trauma creates social outcasts and several forms of psychological neuroses. (1996, p. 35)

I needed to know that I wasn't crazy and I wanted to feel like I belonged again. "The primary wound of trauma is one of disconnection (from self, body, other, life and God). The wound of disconnection must be addressed and healed if victims are ever going to discover wholeness and a life in the Spirit" (Grant, 1996, p. 34). I deeply desired to walk with the Spirit of God once again. I wanted to hear His still quiet voice and to be stilled by His presence. That was one of my most intense desires, to be in God's presence once again. I had no idea how to find my way there.

Therapy and Narratives

With no other options and desperately wanting relief, I continued therapy and began to open myself more and more. I had begun therapy with some trepidation, but being able to tell my story became the source of relief from some of the chaos and pain in my mind. Judith Herman suggests three approaches in the path toward healing trauma. She explains, "Because the traumatic syndromes have basic features in common, the recovery process also follows a common pathway. The fundamental stages of recovery are establishing safety, reconstructing the trauma story, and restoring the connection between survivors and their community" (Herman, 1997, p. 3). In therapy, I began to tell my story again.

Reconstructing the Trauma Story: Many authors discuss the importance of creating a narrative from the story of trauma. Tedeschi and Calhoun state that these narratives of trauma and survival are important to moving beyond the trauma because survivors are forced to confront questions about meaning and trauma as they work out the details of their stories (2007, p. 9). Herman comments that creating narratives allows trauma survivors to review systematically the meaning of the traumatic event(s). In learning to articulate the destruction of the values and beliefs that once were true, the traumatic survivor "stands mute before the emptiness of evil, feeling the insufficiency of any known system of explanation" (Herman, 1997, p. 178). In telling the story and creating meaning, the survivor becomes " a theologian, a philosopher, and a jurist" (Herman, 1997, p. 178).

The benefits of storytelling come from the act of finding meaning within the traumatic events and the aftermath. "Making a story that weaves painful circumstances into a wider framework is an act of hope and faith that is of real benefit both to the individual, their families and wider community" (Walton, 2002, p. 3). Hoge also discusses the benefits of storytelling to the warriors when they return home. Even though the act of storytelling can bring back the same physical reactions that warriors had in the combat zone, the act of storytelling is important on several levels. Narration accomplishes the following:

- Connects emotions and feelings with events so that emotions cease to be walled off from the rest of a warrior's life

- Helps warriors to recognize that they are not alone in their experiences

- Allows warriors to express their emotions and feelings in words

- Allows warriors to speak with someone who is concerned, caring and empathetic as well as professional.

"Of all the different treatments for PTSD that have been tested, the most consistently effective involve narrating the story of the traumatic event(s) in some way so that the story becomes part of who you are" (Hoge, 2010, pp. 116-117). Telling the story is essential to healing for a warrior.

As I began telling my story over the next year, I found that I was able to express all the emotions, pain, and chaos that had been locked deeply inside of me. I spoke of the horror, cried over the deaths, explained my helplessness, and began to feel the presence of God again. I began to find meaning in the events that I had witnessed and experienced in the combat zone. I began to find some release from the chaos in my mind. I found short periods of respite from the war.

Establishing Safety: Kathy and I both read *Once a Warrior, Always a Warrior.* I found so many ideas helpful in the suggestions that Hoge includes to change behaviors and responses. The one that I began to practice at home and with my counselor was in learning how to use "frequency, intensity, and duration" for expressing my emotions. The concept is to lengthen the time between explosive outbursts, to lessen their intensity, and to shorten their duration (Hoge, 2010, p. 85). This approach took much practice and many months before I saw any results. My responses were automatic so I had to learn to change those habits. Outside of therapy, Kathy and I began to have long talks that became deeper and deeper. She listened to me, made suggestions, and accepted me as I was. Yet,

I still had habits to change. The focus on the frequency, intensity, and duration approach is to act in such a way that the responses are "low, mild, and short" (Hoge, 2010, p. 85). Thus, the frequency of emotional expression is low, the intensity is mild, and the duration is short. I repeated the phrase, "low, mild, and short," often so that I could replace my hair-trigger responses with a milder approach.

At this same time, Kathy was creating a safe home for me. Her attempts to maintain a high level of orderliness relieved some of my anxiety. She stopped arguing with me and began to talk to me in terms that I understood. From that, I felt validated. I had not realized how much of an outsider I was in the world that we lived in. Kathy's validation of my experiences, my reactions, my feelings, and my wound told me that I was not crazy, sick, or broken. The shame was starting to subside. It still raised its ugly head occasionally, but it was lessening.

In our talks, Kathy was adamant that I was wounded and that I needed to deal with the wound. I was fearful that when people found out I had PTSD, they would think I was "less than." As I listened to Kathy describe what was happening within me, I felt such relief. I no longer felt alone in a world that considered me crazy. Kathy's questions about how I felt and what I was thinking validated me so much. Her movement from trying to change me to accepting me completely opened the door for me to be able to work at a deeper level with the counselor. Her creation of a safe home empowered me to be able to open up the place inside of me where I had stuffed all of my grief, fear, anger, and other emotions for so long.

These two dynamics for moving toward healing—telling my story and a safe environment—were the elements that caused the bottom to drop out from under me. As I felt safer, I began to peek into the chaos that I kept inside. Then it seemed that I was flooded by all of the emotions that I had stuffed inside all of those years at war and afterwards. I often felt so overwhelmed that I wanted to quit this journey. But I wanted to be free of the shame, guilt, and pain more than I wanted to quit. I continued going to counseling and opening up more and more of the hidden parts of me.

As I went deeper into the pain, I became more and more dependent on Kathy. I was embarrassed by how needy I was, but I knew that she could support me until I found some stability. When I would tell her I was embarrassed, she would remind me that I had a war wound and that I had nothing to be ashamed of. I began to lose control of most areas of my life. I had to ask Kathy if my socks matched my clothes. I couldn't remember the rules anymore. I would ask her to help me with decisions and with other parts of my life that I had always handled. Everything fell apart. Part of me knew that I was asking too much of her at times. I needed her home because I feared the emotions that had been set loose. Kathy made me feel safe and I wanted her nearby when I was home. I leaned on her to help me through this time.

Restoring Connections: Slowly across the months and then years, Kathy and I began to connect on a deeper and deeper level. I worked with the VA VET Center counselor for a little over a year. He then moved and I was transferred to another counselor. I decided to stop going for awhile. I talked this decision out with Kathy before I quit counseling. I realized that we were beginning to connect again as friends and family. I slowly had begun to trust her so that I could begin to open up. Yet, I still felt empty. I struggled to pray and to worship.

I was confused because I had followed the guidelines that most of my counseling and theological books set forth. I was telling my story and feeling safer. Counseling was essential to reaching this stage. I dealt with my mind, body, and emotions. But I still was not at peace. I struggled daily to move beyond my wound. I wanted to break the bonds that the wound had on me. My coping skills were improving. I was able to use strategies more effectively and I was improving.

I began to realize that positive effects were possible and that I might find my way to healing. That knowledge greatly empowered me, but then I would falter. I began to read all that I could find on "resilience," which means "to spring back." Resilience is being able to respond to hard times in a constructive way so that one can "bounce back from adverse experiences and circumstances quickly and effectively" (Berger, 2015, pp. 12-13). I was trying my best to bounce back quickly and effectively; but I was unable to bounce anywhere. I became fearful that the rest of my life would be spent in this halfway state where I was constantly bombarded with traumatic memories with only short spans of relief.

I now know that I had not addressed the spiritual side of my wound. The wound that is labeled "PTSD" is a wound of the body, mind, AND spirit. Finding meaning in trauma is the realm of God, not psychology. While safety and telling my story had brought me temporary peace, I had not addressed the deep wound to my spirit. My relationship with God had not been restored. God was calling me to move deeper in relationship with Him through the traumatic wound that I had received, but I fought the call of the wound. I had to complete several steps of preparation before I could face this wound. I had to cease my continual activity and begin to be at home with myself.

> Human withdrawal is a very painful and lonely process, because it forces us to face directly our own condition in all its beauty as well as misery. When we are not afraid to enter into our own center and to concentrate on the stirrings of our own soul, we come to know that being alive means being loved. This experience tells us that we can only love because we are born out of love, that we can only give because our life is a gift, and that we can only make others free because we are set free by Him whose heart is greater than ours. When we have found the anchor places for our lives in our own center, we can be free to let others enter into the space created for them and allow them to dance their own dance, sing their own song and speak their own language without fear. (Nouwen, 1972, pp. 91-92)

I had to find my own center again. This search required me to release the pent-up emotions that I had shoved inside of myself for so long. I had to continue to lean on Kathy because I had lost all confidence in my own abilities. I had also lost my ability to measure my own reactions. I could no longer determine what was appropriate and what was inappropriate. The most fearful part was having to release control and step out of my self-protective cocoon.

I again was at a place where nothing worked. The fear, guilt, and shame continued to overwhelm me. The chaos in my mind was lessened, but it still was in control of me. Grant remarks, "Spiritually—trauma is a necessity. Most curse their wounds as bad luck or punishment. Few give thanks for their capacity to expand consciousness" (1996, p. 35). I viewed my wounds as a source of shame. I did not understand how I could give thanks for any part of what was happening inside me. What I have come to realize is that we cannot have full communion with God through the Holy Spirit until we walk the way of the wound.

Chapter 9 discusses the journey that took me through the dark night of the soul and brought me to a deeper relationship with God where I found peace, hope, and healing. Before I could find peace and hope, my heart had to change so that I was more sensitive to the movements of the Holy Spirit. The isolation and pain of my wound set me on a long journey of working through the spiritual consequences of my wound. In *The Way of the Wound*, Grant adds, "The Spirit does not speak through words or concepts, but by producing changes in the heart. Every seeker must develop a heart sensitive to the movements of the Spirit. Spiritual ignorance is not overcome by concepts but by experiences" (1996, p. 8) of abandoning old images of God and of ourselves that separate us from God. Instead, we must learn deeper understandings of God through the Holy Spirit (Grant, 1996, p. 8).

I answered the call of the Holy Spirit to walk the way of the wound. I began my journey asking God to protect me wheresoe'er I go.

CHAPTER NINE

"Protect Them Wheresoe'er They Go"

Warriors return from the combat zone wounded in mind and body, but also in spirit. The terms, "Post Traumatic Stress," describes the time period after traumatic stress happens; however, the term, "Disorder," is a psychiatric word that does not actually express the entirety of the woundedness of the warrior. Receiving a PTSD diagnosis generally means that the warrior seeks psychotherapy for a period of time. Usually, the warrior receives some relief because of the ability to voice the story of the traumatic events. Psychotherapy serves an important function in the healing process. Part of the purpose of storytelling, however, is to discover meaning within that narrative. Warriors returning with PTSD must tell their stories, but they also must heal the wound to their spirits. Finding meaning in trauma is a concern of spirituality. Responding to the call of the Holy Spirit to walk the way of the wound is one of the most difficult decisions that warriors—or any trauma survivors—can make.

Many books and articles touch on spirituality's importance to returning warriors. Some suggest that spirituality could help warriors achieve benefits such as increased resilience facing the future, increased meaning or purpose to their lives, and strengthened coping mechanisms amid crises. These books and articles also that address negative views of God, such as "God is punishing me," can be a result of spirituality. The problem of evil and how to deal with it is in the realm of spirituality (Drescher, et al., 2007, pp. 299-303). These approaches recommend spirituality as part of the recovery process, but few encourage the readers to answer the Holy Spirit as it calls us to a new and deeper relationship with God.

In this book, we are approaching spirituality from a Christian perspective that includes the totality of creation. Our spirit is the part of us that answers the call of the Holy Spirit to seek God through His Son, Jesus Christ. It includes our seeking to understand the meaning of events in our lives, particularly traumatic events. The seeking of that which can't be fully known, but must be accepted in faith is a spirituality that stretches back in time through the Christian mystics and into the early church. Henri Nouwen and Robert Grant are two of the authors who do encourage this deeper journey to find healing for spiritual wounds. The concepts of healing that flow from this ideal of spiritual wounds means that authentic seekers find peace, hope, and grace through the wounds. "Healing" doesn't refer to an "all's well" approach or an approach that scratches the surface of our spirituality. Healing spiritual wounds carries us deeper in our relationship to God. Healing that means problems such as PTSD just disappear is not the goal of healing the spiritual wound. Spiritual health is the goal of healing the spiritual wound.

Robert Grant presents a challenge to walk the way of the wound in seeking a spirituality of trauma. As I found relief from the chaos and pain in my mind with the therapist and our safer home, I still was seeking to reestablish a deeper relationship with God. Spiritually, I felt numb and that numbness made me feel empty. My attempts to repair the relationship seemed futile. The old church, the men's groups and similar activities, I know now, were my attempts to avoid the call of the Holy Spirit to enter the wound. I read the Scriptures, but I didn't feel nourished as I always had. Our new church brought me moments of respite, but my spirit was so wounded that I was unable to maintain any semblance of peace.

> The goal of every victim is to wake up and learn the lessons of his/her life as they are called out by experiences that overwhelm his/her familiar ways of coping and making sense....Only by listening to and being guided by the meaning of one's wounds can victims come to know and live fully in the Spirit. There are few paths to the Spirit besides the way of the wound. (Grant, 1996, p. 5)

I made the decision to wake up and learn the lessons of my wounds.

Grant describes the challenging journey that a spirituality of trauma requires. He explains that journeying through the wound demands blood, sweat, and tears from the wounded. In order to overcome the despair and suffering generated by traumatic injuries, victims must discard "cherished versions of self, world and God. Initially, a spirituality of trauma is a spirituality of disillusionment and grief. Ultimately, it can become a spirituality of compassion, liberation and peace" (Grant, 1996, p. 4). As I began to listen to the call of the Spirit to travel through my wound, I found that I was unable to respond. I was so tightly locked inside of myself that I defeated my own attempts at responding to the Spirit. I was clinging to old versions of myself, trying to stay afloat as the ship was sinking.

As a traumatized person, I had learn to "transcend limited versions of [myself] while, at the same time," I had to align myself with something greater. "Most human restlessness and pain is the result of the Spirit's incessant demand that humans live from the deepest part of their being" (Grant, 1996, p. 4). The deepest part of my being, my spiritual self, was the traumatized part of my being. As I began to experience benefits gained from therapy and from the changes in my home, I seemed to slip further away from God in my spiritual life. I prayed and I heard the call of the Spirit, but like most people, I ignored it. The call urged me to loosen the control I had on my life, but that hyper-control had been instrumental in my survival skills. The call urged me to break free from my self-protective casing and stand vulnerable before God.

Jesus heard this call when He was in the Garden of Gethsemane. As He begged God to allow Him another way, Jesus ended with, "Not my will, but Thy will" (Luke 22:39-46). The example of Jesus' submission was a difficult one to follow. Because Jesus submitted to God, He went to the cross to die for all of mankind. The cross was extreme trauma. However, if there was no cross, then there would be no resurrection. If there was no trauma, then there would be no hope (Thomas, "Does the Empty Tomb," 2015).

Paul also heard the call on the road to Damascus. Jesus issued the call to Paul. As a rising star in the Jewish religious and scholarly world, Paul was on a mission to do God's work. He was on his way to kill all of the Christians in Damascus. Leaving Jerusalem breathing threats against Christians, this zealous man was blinded on that road. Christ called him to participate in the Kingdom of God. When Paul rose from the ground, he was blind. This powerful man had to depend on a servant to lead him to Damascus. He was completely vulnerable to anyone and anything. The mission for God that Paul had begun that day ended with a blind, confused Paul entering Damascus. How could he have been so wrong about what God wanted from him? This question had to have been part of the spiritual crisis Paul suffered during those few days. Thus, wounded in body and spirit, Paul spent several days waiting for God to speak through Ananias. After his sight was restored, Paul spent the next three years studying before he ever met with the leaders of the Christian church in Jerusalem. Trauma, in this case, taught a leader that his path was not God's way (Acts 9, Galatians 1).

These examples from the Bible have several things in common. The men in them had become completely vulnerable before God. I knew that I had to do the same, but I struggled with becoming so vulnerable. In order to respond to the Spirit, I had to release all of the control over myself. The wounds of warriors are spiritual as well as mental and physical. My wounded spirit was a part of me that I carefully guarded, protecting it at all costs. I had spent so many years protecting myself—and especially my spirit—that I had forgotten how to live any other way. The Spirit's incessant call, however, continued over the next few years. I tried again and again to respond, but my control over my innermost being won out each time. God would not respond to my telling Him what to do. He continued to demand that I turn control over to Him. I could not do so for several years. I continued in my life of pain and chaos, experiencing momentary respite in church. I could not find a lasting peace and I was unable to find enduring hope.

"I Have Severe PTSD"

In September, 2014, Kathy and I were invited to give a presentation on PTSD for the local chapter of Blue Star Mothers (an organization for mothers whose children are veterans or serving in the military). As we worked up a PowerPoint and some videos, my anxiety grew by the day. All my fears of people finding me "less than," or thinking I was a nut case or judging me were rolled up into this presentation. I kept telling Kathy that we weren't going to say this or that. I wanted to be sure that we didn't do anything to make me appear to be an angry, controlling guy. Kathy argued that everyone with a PTSD family member understands what the wound involves and they understand how warriors act when they return with PTSD. While that might be true, I didn't want to be presented like that.

During the week before the presentation, my anxiety grew enormously. I began to practice saying, "I am Captain Mike Langston and I have been diagnosed with severe PTSD." I told Kathy that I was going to open by saying, "I am Captain Mike Langston and I have been diagnosed with severe PTSD." Kathy said that was fine. About the sixth time I told her, she asked me why I kept telling her that.

I explained how much anxiety I felt. In all of my explaining, Kathy understood that those words were more than what they appeared to be. This gathering would be the first time I stood in front of a group of people and said that I have PTSD. My anxiety grew each day. I began thinking of ways to get out of the presentation, but I knew that I couldn't. After all, I was the one who had agreed to it!

On the evening of the presentation, I wore my uniform. I felt good wearing it again. We had to wait through three other speakers and I felt my anxiety growing. One of the speakers was from a local mental health association. She kept saying, "PTSD is a mental illness," "PTSD is a mental illness," "PTSD is a mental illness." Her major point was our need to de-toxify the term "mental illness" so that those with PTSD can better accept the inevitable. Kathy told me later that she almost stood up and took the mike from the woman several times. She also said that the woman was lucky that she didn't have a fist in her mouth, because she made Kathy so angry. There was my five-foot, three-inch wife talking about fighting. It was a humorous image!

Finally, the three speakers finished and it was our turn. Our daughter, a college freshman who lived nearby, came in shortly before we started. As we were introduced, we stood up, turned on our PowerPoint, and I found myself in front of the microphone. I had told Kathy that I would begin with the words and then she could present most of the rest of the meeting.

I stood there for a moment as my anxiety took over my mind. I was nearing panic as I tried to remember what I was going to say. I kept thinking of what those people in the audience would say when I said I had severe PTSD. After what seemed like a long time (but was actually less than a minute), I opened my mouth and "My name is Captain Mike Langston and I have been diagnosed with severe PTSD" came out. I was not prepared for what happened next.

A tremendous feeling of relief washed over me as I stood there. No one reacted like I thought they would. They were attentive and compassionate. None of my earlier fears happened. People just accepted the statement and that was it. More importantly, however, is the freedom that stating those words gave me.

Saying those simple words in front of that audience empowered me greatly. It was my first public announcement of my diagnosis. Much of the shame and embarrassment left me with that open announcement. I was so relieved by my ownership of the diagnosis.

Even though I had told Kathy to talk most of the time, I took over the talking and eagerly presented. When we finished, the people in the crowd talked with me and were supportive. Most of them shared stories—their own from Vietnam, Afghanistan, Iraq, or from their children—about PTSD. This event was a watershed event in my healing process. This admission opened the door for me to begin to tell others that I have been diagnosed with moderate to severe PTSD. I still felt some shame, but it was no longer the major emotion driving my life.

Spiritual Wound

Releasing the shame that had hampered me for years was instrumental in my ability to answer the call of the Holy Spirit to enter the wound to my spirit. Westerners usually deny the need to respond to traumatic events as a wound to the spirit. Instead, people in the Western world seek immediate relief and a rapid return to a "normal" life. Thus, Westerners experience trauma that undermines all of their beliefs in life, God, and people. They face evil and become aware of how vulnerable their lives really are. Instead of turning to the Holy Spirit to lead them, Westerners tend to take medications, abuse alcohol or other addictive substances, perform destructive behaviors, or fill their lives with frantic activities. These behaviors and others insulate the person, momentarily offsetting the pain and chaos of the trauma. These choices, however, provide no lasting relief to the trauma victim (Grant, 1996, p. 9).

A modern focus for warriors with a PTSD wound is to find a "new normal." Normal requires people to live in denial that people throughout the world, their country, their state, their city, their neighborhood, and often, their home are experiencing evil firsthand through a myriad of ways. "Western consciousness worships the ego and its ideal of self-sufficiency....Self-sufficiency denies all truths that transcend self-interest" (Grant, 1996, pp. 40-41). Choosing a "new normal" as the goal of recovery means that warriors have to return to some state that mimics the warriors' pre-traumatized worlds. Inserting the word, "normal," into any phrase discussing recovery or healing from a PTSD wound implies that warriors can set aside their traumatic memories and experiences and live as innocently as they did before they encountered such evil. This goal negates warriors' sacrifices and additionally, does not draw warriors into a deeper experience with God. Similar to how we deal with a broken leg, we, as a society, deal with warriors' spiritual recovery hoping that they can find that "new normal" that will make them as "good as new in no time." We then have no more responsibility for warriors.

Warriors throughout our society, however, are living with wounded spirits that will never be "good as new." Nor should that be the goal for warriors or those who know, live with, or work with warriors. Their experiences of trauma have changed their minds, bodies, emotions, and spirits. The up-tempo pace can be slowed down and the automatic responses can become thought-out responses—at least, for most of the time. Bodies can be repaired or can be accommodated. Spirits, however, can only be reached through the wound itself.

Realizing that God calls to warriors to deepen their relationship with Him through their wounds should be a signal to us to reach these warriors by providing them with a way to find God and to do it through their traumatic experiences. Grant challenges our society to care for victims of trauma when he writes, "Yet it is usually unresolved trauma that *demands* more comprehensive approaches to God and self....The discovery of meaning is usually left to the victim. A spirituality of trauma has the potential to recover what has been personally and culturally disowned" (1996, p. 9). Warriors know that not only their minds and bodies are traumatized by war, but their spirits are as well.

Authentic Seeker: In order to begin the journey through spiritual wounds, people must desire to be an authentic seeker of God. This term means that the seekers seek the guidance, power, wisdom, and love of God through His Son, Jesus Christ. The earthly Comforter that Christ left after His resurrection is the Holy Spirit (John 15:26-16:15). The Holy Spirit draws us to God through His Son, Jesus Christ. Those desiring the authentic development that the Spirit offers must reject our current social reality that "promises happiness in exchange for the denial and suppression of certain personal and existential truths. Acceptance of this pact severely reduces any chance of authentic development" (Grant, 1996, p. 34). Thus, to be an authentic seeker, we must reject the concept of "normality" in all of its forms and accept our wounds and the truths within them. "The way of the wound demands that images of God emerge out of personal experience and critical reflection" (Grant, 1996, p. 9). We focus so little energy on the critical reflection requirement of seeking God.

The trauma victim who becomes an authentic seeker strives to "discover healing and direction in events that not only injure but which have the power to destroy. How to develop hope and spiritual deepening in the midst of despair is a challenge that every survivor must meet" (Grant, 1996, p. 3). The concept of developing hope and spiritual deepening in the midst of despair is counter-intuitive to most approaches offered in our current society. The authentic seeker who has been traumatized learns that "many profound spiritual transformations occur when one is forced, through pain, to abandon beliefs that prevent one from embracing the spiritual center of his/her consciousness" (Grant, 1996, p. 4). Pain can be a path to the Holy Spirit, but we tend to avoid pain in our culture.

To become an authentic seeker, warriors must first abandon the intense self-protection that served them so well in the combat zone. This step is not a simple one. To abandon those protective actions means that warriors expose themselves on all sides. The anxiety created by this action borders on panic. I spent several years offering to open part of myself while, at the same time, maintaining control over the other parts of me. The Holy Spirit would not accept my partial offering. Many Scriptural examples exist of tainted offerings from Cain offering less than the best (Genesis 4:1-16) to the offerings of the rich compared to the widow giving all she had (Luke 21:1-4). I had read these stories countless times and preached on them as well, but I wasn't able to fully offer myself because I was still in self-protection mode. Initiation into the deeper realms of the Holy Spirit "often involves being wounded and then a long process of working through the consequences of these wounds" (Grant, 1996, p. 8).

As the months went by, I struggled to release control of the self-protective mode I had lived in for so many years. I deeply desired to become an authentic seeker. "All seekers need to come under the guidance, power, wisdom and love of the Spirit. Ultimately this means developing a fuller, more conscious and heart-felt connection to the Source of life. Initially, spirituality is a way of knowing. Eventually, it must become a way of being" (Grant, 1996, p. 8). I struggled to release the control unaware that my desire to become an authentic seeker was a desire that allowed the Spirit to begin healing me. I did, however, know what my goal was. "The authentic seeker longs for more than just peak experiences or spiritual highs. S/he desires to live in and be transformed by the Spirit, while overcoming anything that separates him/her from the Spirit" (Grant, 1996, p. 8). I became more aware of attitudes of my heart that were separating me from God.

Even though the path to becoming an authentic seeker differs from person to person, I have formulated several steps that are essential to that pursuit. These steps, while general in nature, can assist those warriors—and others—seeking a way to begin in the midst of the chaos and pain that can overwhelm them. The Holy Spirit, however, leads authentic seekers on the journeys that God chooses. The steps are as follows:

1. Begin by praying multiple times a day, asking God to show you how to become an authentic seeker and to give you courage to move from a self-protective state.

2. After you pray, LISTEN to God's responses.

3. Read Scriptures. Psalms contains many chapters in which the Psalmist cries out to God for relief. These Psalms can bring comfort by giving words to the agonies within our souls. They can become warriors' prayers as well.

4. Reject current social realities that a "quick fix" exists and that a "new normal" is just around the corner. The journey to spiritual health is long and strenuous.

5. Begin to accept that pain and trauma are paths to a deeper relationship with God. Embrace spiritual pain and trauma as paths to the Holy Spirit.

6. Understand that lasting relief only comes when you accept that deep spiritual meanings can be learned through your wounds. It will be difficult to find lasting relief from the pain.

7. Attempt to embrace the spiritual center of your being. This particular step requires the help of the Holy Spirit who draws us to God. Add this to your prayer.

8. Work to abandon self-protection. This step requires a safe environment and a trusted friend or counselor to stand beside you. The vulnerability you feel

can overwhelm you even with support. Have faith that God is there.

Opening to the Spirit: As time passed, I began to be more and more comfortable out of my protective shell. I continued praying for guidance and for strength to loosen my control; however, I maintained control of my innermost spiritual self. This wounded part of me was the part that I protected the most. Kathy and I continued deepening our relationship. In church, I began to feel the Holy Spirit more and more. The respite I found on Sunday mornings began lasting a bit longer; however, I still was not fully open to the moving of the Spirit within me.

In February 2015, I spent seven weeks in Germany, teaching two graduate classes for a German seminary in Stuttgart. This time alone with none of my usual activities and few people to talk to served as a time of healing for me. I prayed often, read extensively, wrote many pages, and reflected deeply on Scripture and other writings. I was unaware of it at the time, but I became more at peace with myself than I had been since before I went to war—nine and a half years. On the phone, Kathy and I had begun to talk about Robert Grant's book, *The Way of the Wound*, which she was rereading. She began to remind me of the concepts within the book that included turning to face our wounds and trusting the Holy Spirit to guide us through the wounds. I heard her, but I knew that I was not strong enough to do that yet.

When I returned to the safety of home and church, I suddenly found myself surrounded by teaching and Scripture that discussed the spiritual journey that I was avoiding. Kathy had pulled out notes from a sermon on Psalm 23 that she was reviewing for this book. As I began reading the notes from that sermon, I also opened my Bible to read the Scripture. Psalm 23, can be divided into four parts which describe the Shepherd as performing the following tasks: protects, provides, is present, and pursues us. "The Lord is my Shepherd/I shall not want" speaks to God providing us with what we need. "He makes me lie down in green pastures/He leads me besides still waters" continues this theme of providing for our needs. Sheep need grass and water to stay alive and our Shepherd provides for our needs (Thomas, "A Very Scottish Psalm," 2014).

The next section of Psalm 23 stood out from the rest. "He restores my soul." I desperately wanted my soul restored. From the depth of my self-protective mode, my spirit responded to the promise of God restoring my soul. The following verse, however, seemed more of a promise of times to come: "He leads me in the paths of righteousness for His name's sake." I wasn't sure about where I was in relationship to "righteousness" but I found myself desiring to be led by the Shepherd. I had known the path of righteousness. I desired to find this path again. A glimmer of hope flickered in my protected spirit.

I had been following the steps that I listed for finding my authentic self for several months. I had prayed for the Spirit to lead me, to help me accept my spiritual wound, and to lead me to a deeper relationship with God. The next verses touched me at the deepest levels of my soul. I recoiled from them; yet, I was drawn to them. "Yea, though I walk through the valley of the shadow of death,/ I will fear no evil; for Thou art with me./ Thy rod and thy staff they comfort me." Suddenly, all of my danger and high threat physical reactions were going off. My heart was racing, adrenaline was rushing through my blood, and I was beginning to panic. Those verses filled me with fear and panic. I realized that the Holy Spirit was calling to me through my wound. I had to walk through the valley of the shadow of death.

I had already walked among so much death, how could I possibly be able to walk through this valley? I had already been there in real life and then in my dreams. My anxiety levels continued to rise. I felt completely unprotected. I tried to reel my spirit back in but it seemed to be out of control. Return to the valley of the shadow of death? I couldn't do that.

My vision dropped to my Bible. There the words of Psalm 23 seemed to rise from the page. "For Thou art with me." I saw those words as a promise from God. If I chose to walk through this valley of the shadow of death—my spiritual wound—then I would not necessarily have this incredible fear of evil. The Holy Spirit would walk with me and God's rod and staff would comfort me. I knew from my previous studies that the Shepherd's rod and staff were the instruments that kept the sheep on the right path. In this verse, God was saying that if I entered this valley of the shadow of death, I did not need to be afraid. He said that He would keep me on the path with His rod and staff. Most importantly, He said He would be with me.

When I calmed down enough to read the notes again, I remembered the references to the sickness of our spirits. This sickness blocks our abilities to experience the table that God prepares before us (Thomas, "A Very Scottish Psalm," 2014). "You prepare a table before me in the presence of my enemies/You anoint my head with oil; my cup runs over." I knew that my self-protective state was preventing me from experiencing this table that God provides. It was the next part of the verse, however, that pierced my spirit. God prepares a table for us *in the presence of our enemies*. The table isn't far away or sheltered, but it sits in the middle of our enemies. My enemies were numerous and included self-protection, control, chaos, pain, and other struggles that I was clinging to. David knew much of war and its aftermath. His Psalm was stating that this table of God's was in the midst of the chaos and pain. The table was not set in a tranquil setting. This insight overwhelmed me.

The final part of Psalm 23, "Surely goodness and mercy will follow me all the days of my life;/And I will dwell in the house of the Lord forever," explains that God pursues us. He corrals us with goodness and mercy. The cost of that, however, is that we cast our spirit on God. Healing comes only if we surrender our innermost being completely to God (Thomas, "A Very Scottish Psalm," 2014).

I knew as I finished reading Psalm 23 that I had a decision to make. I had to decide whether I wanted my spirit to be healed.

This healing of my spirit required me to open my spirit totally to God, to move out of my self-protective state and to give up control. "Human care, in conjunction with divine assistance, are what enable individuals to develop to the point where their egos become strong enough to step aside and allow the deeper dimensions of the Self to emerge" (Grant, 1996, p. 13). I had the tools necessary to enter the valley of the shadow of death. My desperation to be free from these bonds of self-protection and control brought me to the point where I prayed for God to heal all of me.

Dark Night of the Soul: Strong winds blow constantly in Iceland. A day without wind is a rare day. The winds blow steadily throughout the day at about thirty-five knots. Gusts normally reach fifty or sixty knots. Winds can blow much stronger than that but the normal day is very windy.

In Iceland, we lived at the top of a small cliff from which we could see the North Atlantic waves hit the coastal cliffs near Keflavik. When I finished my daily runs, I would go to the cliff to watch the sea. When storms were coming in, the waves would pound the cliffs with tremendous energy. The winds would gust at eighty to ninety knots. The power in the waves and the wind was invigorating.

When these powerful storms were blowing in, I began to wonder if the wind would hold me. It could blow me around if the storm was powerful enough, but could it hold me up? One day, I walked near the edge of the cliff I was on and leaned forward. The wind held me. I didn't fall but instead, I was close to "flying with my feet still on the ground." Each time I moved closer to the cliff's edge. One day, I went to the furthest edge that I could. I stood for a moment and then leaned forward as far as I could into the wind. I looked straight down at the ground at the bottom of the cliff. I was suspended in space. It was one of the most invigorating experiences that I have had. This act required me to have complete trust that the wind would continue blowing and that I would be held up by the wind. Otherwise, I would have fallen down a steep cliff and my body would have shattered. I was held up that first day and many days after that. Total trust and total commitment were the tools I needed for this experience.

Walter Brueggemann, in *Spirituality of the Psalms,* divides many of the Psalms into three areas of concentration: "psalms of orientation, psalms of disorientation, and psalms of new orientation" (2002, p. 8). Brueggemann explains these ideas with "Human life consists in satisfied seasons of wellbeing that evoke gratitude for the constancy of blessing" (2002, p. 8). These periods of orientation produce feelings of "joy, delight, goodness, coherence, and reliability of God, God's creation, and God's governing law" (Brueggemann, 2002, p. 8). Psalms of disorientation express the emotions of "anguished seasons of hurt, alienation, suffering, and death. These evoke rage, resentment, self-pity, and hatred" (Brueggemann, 2002, p. 8). I realized that I had been living in this period of disorientation spiritually which affected my physical and mental life as well.

"Human life consists in turns of surprise when we are overwhelmed with the new gifts of God, when joy breaks through the despair. Where there has been only darkness, there is light" (Brueggemann, 2002, pp. 8-9). This new orientation represents leaving the pit of despair and chaos when we have decided that we will never escape this pit. Brueggemann argues, "It is a departure inexplicable to us, to be credited only to the intervention of God. This move of departure to new life includes a rush of positive responses, including delight, amazement, wonder, awe, gratitude, and thanksgiving" (2002, p. 11). This movement into a new orientation is a movement that God controls and we respond to His calling.

I know that it was March or April. Maybe it was May of 2015. I can't tell you when it started or when it ended. I only can share what I remember. A long tunnel stretched out in front of me. Somehow, I knew I was to enter it. I knew that the tunnel contained the valley of the shadow of death. I'm not sure how I knew, but I was positive that the valley was in the tunnel. I could hear the Spirit calling to me out of that tunnel. The call touched the innermost part of my soul. At first, I recoiled from it, struggling not to flip into my self-protective mode. I felt so vulnerable. "The most difficult challenge is to bear the anxiety that accompanies being vulnerable" (Grant, 1996, p. 94). I felt so alone. "Taking the reflective turn and moving into pain and nothingness is the ultimate act" of courage (Grant, 1996, p. 93). "At this point in the journey every victim has acknowledged that there is a problem and that something must change. Yet suspicion, fear, shame and pain inhibit each step" (Grant, 1996, pp. 94-95). Doubt is always there as is ambivalence and anxiety. Victims are asked to consciously embrace their suffering. Divine aid is needed to move us through this phase so my prayers increased. I knew that my challenge was "to move beyond the surface dimensions of [my] wound" (Grant, 1996, p. 95); however, the greatest reason for my movement was this statement from Grant (1996): "Where there is danger there is also salvation" (95). I wanted to be saved from this chaotic pain that was preventing my spiritual wound from finding peace, hope, and healing.

As I stood at the entrance to that tunnel, the call of the Spirit was filled with so much love and promise. There was a promise of healing in the call. There was peace and hope in that call. I stood on the edge of the long tunnel and waited. I knew what I had to do, but I needed more time. I needed more courage. I needed less self-protection. I needed to surrender control. I waited a bit more. Then I realized that if I waited until I was ready, I would never enter the tunnel. Fear and chaos were crowding my brain. The Spirit continued to call me.

I leaned forward into the tunnel, just as I had leaned into the wind in Iceland. I leaned forward with my total being. As soon as I did, I felt the Holy Spirit reach into the tunnel and begin to pull me through. Someone came alongside me and kept saying, "I am with you. Keep going." I heard that over and over. The horrors, death, and dreams that had haunted me were lining the tunnel. I knew they were there, but my focus remained on the Spirit as I was drawn through this tunnel, hearing God say, "I am with you. Keep going."

Suddenly, I was out. I looked around me and everything was the same. I looked inside of me and everything was different. I was exhausted physically and spiritually, but I was filled with peace and hope that I had not felt in years. I realized that I had just experienced what Christians have historically termed, "the dark night of the soul." This dark night of the soul appears in many places within Scripture. Jacob wrestles with an angel (Genesis 32:22-31), David repents after realizing his sin (Psalm 51), Jesus prays in Gethsemane (Matthew 36: 26-56), Job experiences extreme trauma (Book of Job) and many more examples. I was changed. I began to feel hope again. My spirit was at peace. Most of all, the chaos in my mind was settling. God had answered my prayers by giving me a respite from the war.

The journey had been long, but I knew I had followed the Holy Spirit to spiritual health. I knew this deeply in my spirit. Jesus tells us again and again that we must be like little children in order to enter the Kingdom of God. This concept of vulnerability and helplessness is the core of the path to peace and hope through the Holy Spirit.

In order to travel this journey, authentic seekers can follow some simple steps. These steps differ from person to person, but these steps can help those seeking God's peace and healing to find their way to the path so that the Holy Spirit then can lead them. The steps that begin the journey are as follows:

1. Become an authentic seeker (see above)

2. Continue praying and reflecting on what God is telling you through Scriptures and other people.

3. Listen to God as He begins to guide you.

4. Continue working on loosening control on your self-protection.

5. When the Holy Spirit begins to call to you, respond. Be courageous enough to be vulnerable.

6. Allow the Spirit to lead you on this journey.

No steps exist that work as a temporary fix or a quick fix. The journey through traumatic wounds is long and challenging, but the rewards are tremendous.

Resilience and Posttraumatic Growth (PTG)

Developing in the 1970's, resilience theory focuses on understanding how some people "defy the odds, thrive, and become successful in spite of adverse personal, familial, and environmental circumstances whereas others do not" (Berger, 2015, p. 26). This theory shifted the focus of traditional psychological perspectives from that of pathology (sickness) to that of recovery and well-being. Models of resilience share three common assumptions:

- "Resilience is different than recovery"

- Resilience "is a common phenomenon"

- "There are many paths to resilience" (Berger, 2015, p. 26).

In current studies, scholars argue over whether resilience is "a personal trait, a dynamic process, a capacity, or an outcome of successfully bounding back from adversity" (Berger, 2015, p. 31). While good books and articles present resilience in positive ways, we are choosing to avoid the discussion on the term and the theory for reasons summarized in the following:

> Resilience as a construct has traditionally lacked a consistent, complete and measurable definition. Such definitional ambiguity has partly contributed to the term being incorrectly applied and as a result, asymptomatic individuals are often deemed resilient. Moreover, what were previously known as treatment and training have been renamed "resilience building." At best, such relabeling might reduce the stigma of traditional mental health treatment. At worst, an expanding use of the term may confound a growing database of evidence-based factors that really do differentiate those who do bounce back from stress from those who don't. (Ballenger-Brown, 2010)

The term, "resilience," has become a buzzword in many circles in today's world. Much of what we have read on resilience fails to distinguish trauma from hard times. Concepts that allow people to "spring back" after a rough time are generally useless to those exposed to extreme trauma. Additionally, the way of the wound requires one to appear vulnerable, totally dependent on God. When we appear before Him in this manner, He chooses when He will approach us. God decides the journey and God decides the time. We can't control any of it. "Back" is not where this journey takes us. "Forward" is the direction of this journey.

Moral injury is another approach to PTSD that has gained popularity in recent years. Though the research is limited and the field is new, researchers have proposed a definition and some symptoms for "moral injury." The U.S. Department of Veterans Affairs publishes a quarterly research journal. An article, "Moral Injury in Veterans of War," defines "moral injury" as "an act of serious transgression that leads to serious inner conflict because the experience is at odds with core ethical and moral beliefs" (Maguen & Litz, 2012, p. 1). They continue, "More specifically, moral injury has been defined as perpetrating, failing to prevent, bearing witness to, or learning about acts that transgress deeply held moral beliefs and expectations" (Maguen & Litz, 2012, p. 1). The symptoms of moral injury are similar to the symptoms of PTSD. Maguen and Litz argue that symptoms such as "shame, guilt, demoralization, self-harm," etc. are moral injury, but are not symptoms of PTSD (2012, p. 1). We disagree with this separation.

In "Moral Injury and Psycho-Spiritual Development: Considering the Developmental Context," Harris, et al., describe moral injury with the same "constellation of symptoms" that Maguen and Litz use. Harris, et al., explains that moral injury results "from actions, inactions, or witnessing of events that challenge deeply held moral beliefs or values" (Harris, et al., 2015, p. 1). The descriptions of moral injury are closely related to PTSD; however, moral injury can occur without PTSD resulting. Moral injury refers to warriors experiencing a moral dilemma such as compromising their views on life or death, dealing with civilians in ways that can disturb warriors, and other happenings. Warriors can deal with moral injuries without developing PTSD. Moral injury encourages viewing warriors' experiences as spiritual problems because research shows that combat veterans regard seeking assistance from chaplains as more acceptable than seeking help from mental health providers (Harris, et al., 2015, p. 2). Moral injury, in some cases, is a disturbing event that causes a moral crisis that can lead to PTSD-like symptoms. For others, moral injury is almost synonymous with PTSD.

"Moral injury" is a better term for PTSD since healing can be a result of being morally injured. Post traumatic stress disorder, however, contains the term, "disorder," which implies that the mind will always respond to the disorder. Moral injury is a popular term, but has not yet replaced "PTSD" in technical usage. While moral injury is a concept that can be adapted for our purposes, we have chosen to use the terminology "PTSD" to reflect the diagnostic terminology used at the time of writing. Moral injury is being addressed at this time, but it is not being used as a recognized therapeutic diagnosis.

Posttraumatic growth (PTG) is another trend that is popular today. I found many of the concepts within PTG to be helpful, but like other ideas, this theory doesn't approach the spiritual wound that trauma leaves behind. Tedeschi and Calhoun define posttraumatic growth (PTG) as

> ...the experience of individuals whose development, at least in some areas, has surpassed what was present before the struggle with crises occurred. The individual has not only survived, but has experienced changes that are viewed as important, and that go beyond what was the previous status quo. Posttraumatic growth is not simply a return to baseline—it is an experience of improvement that for some persons is deeply profound. (Tedeschi & Calhoun, 2004, p. 4).

They continue defining PTG by stating that growth is not the result of trauma. Growth comes from the individual's "struggle with the new reality in the aftermath of trauma that is crucial in determining the extent to which posttraumatic growth occurs" (2004, p. 5). Tedeschi and Calhoun caution that PTG doesn't remove the pain or distress and those who experience PTG do not embrace the crisis, trauma, or loss as desirable. "The events themselves, however, are not viewed as desirable—only the good that has come out of having to face them" (Tedeschi & Calhoun, 2004, p. 7). This process, like Grant's way of the wound, is a long process. PTG results in a changed sense of self, changed relationships, and changed philosophy of life (Tedeschi & Calhoun, 2007, pp. 7-11).

While I had grown from the trauma, I did not find a respite from the war until I admitted my spiritual wound. PTG is an excellent beginning model, but the avoidance of the spirit part of humans leaves this model lacking. Mind and body take precedence over spirituality, just as spirituality has taken a back seat in our culture. In Grant's development of the way of the wound, the journey one must take to find new spiritual truths from the traumatic events expands the concepts of PTG. Grant focuses on the need to embrace the wound and to find the Spirit within the wound. Posttraumatic growth has to encompass spirituality for warriors to find spiritual health.

Henri Nouwen also develops this concept in his book, *The Wounded Healer*. Nouwen describes, the "wound of loneliness" that is in our society is "a deep incision in the surface of our existence which has become an inexhaustible source of beauty and self-understanding" (1972, p. 84). Nouwen portrays the wounds we receive from trauma as opportunities for spiritual growth if we allow God to lead us. Nouwen along with many other Christian writers seeks the presence of God, the warmth of the Spirit, and the communion with Christ instead of quick fixes and easy answers. He knows that true peace, hope, and grace have their source in the Father, not on this earth.

The peace that I received is a peace that is given to us through a relationship with Jesus Christ. We don't receive peace from the circumstances in our life, but instead, peace is a gift given to us. Peace is not an absence of hard times or of traumatic events. Peace is an inner circumstance that gives us tranquility. The word, *shalom*, in Hebrew encompasses the concept of our total well-being. God bestows this peace. We find it through prayer, faith, truth, presence, and grace (Duncan, 2015). It is through prayer and faith that we are able to find the courage to approach the dark night of the soul so that the Holy Spirit can minister to us. Understanding that truth is the way of God and can't be found through intellect or any other way is necessary to the quest for peace. It is through the presence of God, Christ, and the Holy Spirit that we feel this peace. Grace is provided to us by Christ's traumatic experience on the cross. Christ walked the way of the wound before us and we can follow His steps as we find our way to peace. Without the cross, there would be no resurrection; without Christ's trauma, we would have no hope.

I never thought I would find hope again. The images that continually rolled through my mind and the constant self-protection was a state of being that I thought would last the remainder of my life. In that state, I had no hope. As I read Nouwen's book about Christian ministers, I realized that my wound had deep meaning. That meaning provided me with hope and that hope was the instrument by which I was able to find a respite from the war. Nouwen writes:

> Hope prevents us from clinging to what we have and frees us to move away from the safe place and enter unknown and fearful territory. This might sound romantic, but when a man enters with his fellow man into his fear of death and is able to wait for him right there, "leaving the safe place" might turn out to be a very difficult act of leadership. It is an act of discipleship in which we follow the hard road of Christ, who entered death with nothing but bare hope. (Nouwen, 1972, p. 77)

From my journey into my spiritual wound, I found hope again through the care, peace, love, and grace given to me by the Holy Spirit. I again found my reason for being on earth. I am able to leave the safe places of our world and walk with those who are seeking a respite from the war. I can wait as they enter these spiritual places. I am not "healed" in the limited way of our world. I still have bad dreams at times. When helicopters pass overhead, I still respond by reaching for my ready kit. I have times when I am again in the combat zone.

Overall, however, I have emotions that fit the situation. My meter for anger works again. The most important part of this journey has been my way through my wound to spiritual health. My relationship with God is flourishing. I am at peace and I have hope. Walking through this wound brought me peace and hope. I now have a ministry that is a healing service. Nouwen summarizes it when he says:

> For a deep understanding of his own pain makes it possible for him to convert his weakness into strength and to offer his own experience as a source of healing to those who are often lost in the darkness of their own misunderstood sufferings. This is a very hard call, because for a minister who is committed to forming a community of faith, loneliness is a very painful wound, which is easily subject to denial and neglect. But once that pain is accepted and understood, a denial is no longer necessary, and ministry can become a healing service. (1972, p. 87)

I spent several years struggling with the after-effects of war. When I finally embraced my traumatic wound, I found my weakness turning to strength and the chaos in my spirit being replaced with peace and hope. I experienced freedom from shame, guilt, pain, and self-protection. As a result, I am able to offer my journey as a source of healing to those who are still trapped in the chaos of war's after-effects. God provided me with peace for my wild confusion. And He will for you as well.

CHAPTER TEN

"And Give, for Wild Confusion, Peace"

"Thus nothing can be written about ministry without a deeper understanding of the ways in which the minister can make his own wounds available as a source of healing" (Nouwen, 1972, p. xvi). Nouwen's words express my reasons for sharing this story of journeying through my wounds. My deepest desire is that others can find a source of healing through reading my journey to spiritual health. "Thus ministry can indeed be a witness to the living truth that the wound, which causes us to suffer now, will be revealed to us later as the place where God intimated his new creation" (Nouwen, 1972, p. 95-96). Kathy and I have not reached a "new normal" in our journeys, but we have discovered that we are new creations with a deeper knowledge of our eternal Father and His presence in our lives.

Kathy: Our home has moved from a place focused on safety to a place full of laughter, teasing, and loving with minor incidents of irritability (from me as often as Mike). Our home remains safe, and as a result, we both enjoy peace and hope. I am awed by the courage my husband exhibited as he embarked on his journey. I admire his persistence in continuing to respond to the Holy Spirit's guidance as he moved bit-by-bit to spiritual health. I watched his struggle to trust again and to move out of his self-protection. His journey was not rapid, but he has found release from the after-effects of war. There are still times that he moves into combat mode: when he hears helicopter blades, he jumps up to meet it; when someone enters our yard rapidly, he jumps up to protect me from the intruder; when a loud unexpected noise happens, he reacts more rapidly than others; or when he is overly-stressed, he can overreact. But when I am overly-stressed, I overreact also. Mike is able to dial his reactions up and dial his reactions down in ways that allow him to control his reactions.

To me, however, the greatest indicator of the changes in our home lies in my health. In the years that Mike struggled to control the after-effects of war on his own, I had a flare-up of rheumatoid arthritis three or four times a year. When I have a flare-up, I have to limit my activities for three or four weeks, and then I can take up to two more months before I am over the flare-up. In other words, I spent more time recovering from flare-ups than living my life. My flare-ups were caused in large part by the intense stress in our household. As of this writing, I have not had a flare-up of rheumatoid arthritis for two years. The long journey over many years has brought Mike to a place of spiritual health. With his spiritual healing, my physical health has improved.

My prayer is that those of you who live with warriors struggling with the after-effects of war can find peace and hope. I also pray for strength for each of you as you support your warrior in the journey to spiritual health. May God, our Father, lead each of you on your journeys into the dark night of the soul.

Mike: I have moved from a place of wild confusion to a place of hope and peace. I have become a minister called to recognize the sufferings of my own times. PTSD exists in many homes and in many lives. Having lived with severe PTSD and having listened to Kathy and my kids as they explain the effects my PTSD has had on them has allowed me to become aware of the struggles of the families that provide love and care to those warriors with PTSD. Most of all though, I have become aware that PTSD is "the starting point of my service." My service to God—my ministry—is only authentic when "it comes from a heart wounded by the suffering" about which I speak (Nouwen, 1972, p. xvi).

The question that rises from the deepest place in our spirit when we experience the trauma of the combat zone echoes the question of the existential crisis: Who am I now? The question of the traumatized spirit, however, is a cry to God: Who am I now in relationship to God? Asking that question is the beginning step to journeying to hope. Wrestling with the chaos and confusion in our minds can make us feel that God has turned away from us or that He doesn't exist. That line of thought is futile for seeking hope and peace. Learning step-by-step to become an authentic seeker will lead us further into the way of the wound so that we can find healing for our spiritual wound.

Nouwen reminds us that living our lives like Christ lived His means that we live our lives as authentically as He lived His. We don't stand to the side like observers (1972, p. 99), but instead, we totally surrender our control, self-protection, and all that we are to the Holy Spirit. We seek God, no matter if the path takes us to Gethsemane and the cross. We know from Christ's example that the cross led to the resurrection, a conquering of death. The resurrection led to hope. Without the trauma of the cross, we never would have the hope that the resurrection has provided to us. Thus, we who are traumatized by war must find ourselves in Gethsemane praying, "Not my will, but Thy will." We must, as Christ did, surrender all control to God and then follow the path He lays out for us. The journey through the wound is the most difficult journey I have ever taken. It is a journey that I highly recommend to all of those seeking relief from the chaos inside your spirit from PTSD. There is peace and hope on the other side of the journey.

I don't have a formula or an easy way out of the traumatization that warriors suffer. There isn't a quick and easy, happy-face Christian method that can quickly wipe away your pain. There is, however, a journey that begins with prayer, Scripture reading, worship attendance, and surrender that each of us must follow. "When we become aware that we do not have to escape our pains, but that we can mobilize them into a common search for life, those very pains are transformed from expressions of despair into signs of hope" (Nouwen, 1972, p. 93). Awareness and acceptance of my pain was an essential step toward hope and healing.

Brueggemann reminds us that "The dominant ideology of our culture is committed to continuity and success and to the avoidance of pain, hurt, and loss. The dominant culture is also resistant to genuine newness and real surprise. It is curious but true, that *surprise* is as unwelcome as is *loss*. And our culture is organized to prevent the experience of both" (Brueggemann, 2002, p. 14). Thus, when we practice any movement into disorientation or into new orientation, we can find ourselves on the outside of society. Most warriors with PTSD and many without, are experiencing this state of disorientation. They need direction to be able to embrace this disorientation and help finding their way to a new orientation through God, our Father.

Through therapy, I have become much more aware of dialing my responses up or dialing them down. I am not perfect and still can revert back into the combat zone responses, but overall, I have found peace for my spirit. I didn't have peace until I addressed my spiritual health. Without peace, I wasn't able to control my responses as well. My restlessness, shame, and pain continued to control me. Once I decided to answer the call of the Holy Spirit to walk the way of the wound, I then found my way to hope and peace. Once I found my way to hope and peace, I felt the healing in my spirit. The shame and guilt dropped away. My focus was on God and no longer on my self-protection needs.

We still exist in a society that doesn't fully accept that transitioning home doesn't mean we stop being warriors (Hoge, 2010, p. x). Some of our families want us back "the way that we were." We can't be that person that we were before we went to war. We can't erase the sights, smells, people, and horrors that we experienced in the combat zone. We shouldn't erase those memories. We owe it to those who were unable to come back to remember them and their sacrifices. We can, however, find a way to live with those memories so that the memories don't control us.

Seeking help in therapy, finding a trusted friend, and walking the way of the wound will bring you to a more peaceful place. This journey is not a rapid one, but takes years of seeking God and preparing ourselves for the way of the wound. We prepare ourselves and then wait for God to lead us—the easiest, yet most difficult action to perform.

In closing, I also want to challenge those warriors with PTSD to step out of the shame that can come with the diagnosis. PTSD is not a sign of weakness or cowardice. PTSD is a sign that the *intensity* of what you endured or the *proximity* of traumatic events to your location or the *duration* of your time of exposure to trauma caused you to leave the combat zone "locked and loaded." Not all warriors come home in that state. For them, we should be happy. For those of us who do, I encourage you to read the information that corresponds to your "at home" actions (Chapter 6) to understand how PTSD is a reflection of your combat skills. We need to be more vocal about having PTSD and we need to bond with each other for support and for understanding. As Henri Nouwen asserts: "But it is exactly in common searches and shared risks that new ideas are born, that new visions reveal themselves and that new roads become visible" (1972, p. 100). The risk is worth the reward.

I also want to challenge churches to become places that accept the spiritually wounded, the ones who can't find a place in happy-face Christianity. This challenge is to be the church that Christ left on earth, not one that desires only to build its numbers. "A fainthearted church that attempts to thwart its decline in membership only by catering to the perceived sufferings of the comfortable instead of allowing itself to be reformed by those who have suffered genuinely and persistently for such a long time may not have too great a future in a world come of age" (Siemon-Netto, 1990, p. 92). The Holy Spirit is issuing a call to live as authentically as Christ did to churches as well.

God is hope, peace, and love. We do not have to escape from our pain to find that we can journey to Him. Once we journey to Him, then the God of healing transforms our despair into hope. I offer the story of my journey to you as a guide in the hopes that you find the courage to answer the call of the Holy Spirit to journey through your own wounds.

> No minister can save anyone. He can only offer himself as a guide to fearful people. Yet, paradoxically, it is precisely in this guidance that the first signs of hope become visible. This is so because a shared pain is no longer paralyzing but mobilizing, when understood as a way to liberation. When we become aware that we do not have to escape our pains, but that we can mobilize them into a common search for life, those very pains are transformed from expressions of despair into signs of hope. (Nouwen, 1972, p 93)

My wild confusion is now peace and hope. My prayer is that you, too, will find your way to our God of peace and hope.

Below is a suggested prayer for those who are contemplating a journey to hope.

Eternal Father,

I know you are indeed strong to save me from the wounds that plague my spirit, but sometimes the pain is so intense and unbearable.

Give me strength to face my fears, give me endurance to keep going when I feel like quitting, and give me the courage to seek assistance and to walk through this dark night of this wound.

For those I love and cherish, provide them with understanding of what I'm going through. Give them peace and the persistence to stay with me.

O God, be my hope, an everlasting help in times of pain and trouble. Let me feel your presence in this journey and to never forget you are with me.

In your holy name I pray Lord. Amen.

In the finest Navy tradition:
Fair Winds and Following Seas

Appendix A

~

**II Marine Expeditionary Force (Forward) Memorial Service
Invocation
2d Marine Logistic Force Amphitheater
Camp Lejeune, NC
11 April 2008
CAPT Michael W. Langston, CHC, USN**

O God, Creator and Redeemer of all, grant unto this assembly Your divine presence and loving care. We come to honor and pay tribute to men and women who have lost their lives on the field of battle. Many hearts are grieved and the loss is sometime unbearable. So, we call upon You, O Father in heaven, to provide for our grief a sense of healing and comfort that provides a calmness in our hearts.

Eternal Father, there are many questions that arise when death comes to a family's life. Sometimes those questions are hard to answer, but we still ask, "Why… Why my loved one? Why me? Why us?… Help us to hear your compassionate response, and loving care. In the quietness of each of our minds help us to hear the soft words that provide healing, and above all, hope.

We have gathered on this field as family, Lord. Help us to connect and reconnect with the people that are around us. For there are many new names, faces, and circumstances. Bless us as we reach out to each other in this difficult time, cause us to grieve and heal together as family members should. Bind these relationships, forged in adversity, into a bond that is eternal.

In the brightness of this morning sun, may we feel the warmth of your love in our midst. Our prayer is for our hearts to once again be glad, our lives to rejoice, and our eternal being to rest in your hope. To God be the glory now and forever, in His holy name I pray. Amen.

Appendix B

II Marine Expeditionary Force (FWD) Memorial Service Sermon
Blessed are the Peacemakers!
Matthew 5: 3-9
Camp Lejeune, NC
11 April 2008
CAPT Michael W. Langston, CHC, USN

Just a few moments ago, Brigadier General Kessler* read a text from Matthew's Gospel know as the Beatitudes. In that scripture text, verse 9 reads, "Blessed are the Peacemakers... for they shall be called the sons of God."

Peacemaking is a divine work and we are here this morning to pay tribute to peacemakers.

We have come together today from many parts of this great nation to honor these Marines, sailors, and soldiers who have made the ultimate sacrifice in their service to their country. We come together this day as military colleagues, family members, and friends to honor them and to remember their courage and sacrifice.

These men and women were our husbands and wives, sons and daughters, brothers and sisters, and our friends. They laughed with us, loved us, and brought meaning to our lives. Their dedication to duty, however, took them to a land far from here. Each of them went when they were called on, and each of them did the tasks they were trained and required to accomplish.

Their commitment to the ideals of freedom for all men and women no matter where they lived caused them to fight gallantly beside their fellow Marines, sailors, and soldiers. In our country today, this extreme dedication to duty is rarely seen. This unsurpassed commitment to the ideal of freedom is not something that we are normally called upon to display.

There have been times in the history of our country, however, when such dedication and commitment has been seen. These men and women that we honor today, in giving the ultimate sacrifice of their lives, have aligned themselves with the Minute Men at Lexington and Concord, the Marines and sailors at Guadalcanal and Tarawa, the soldiers at the Normandy Beachhead on D Day, and all of those brave men and women who have given their lives in the cause of freedom.

The words on the American chapel in Normandy speak of this commitment, dedication, and sacrifice that were displayed by those landing at Normandy and that have again been displayed through the men and women of II Marine Expeditionary Force (Forward) in Iraq. The words say:

> These endured all and gave all that justice among nations might prevail and that mankind might enjoy freedom and inherit peace.

Through their dedication, commitment, and sacrifice, these men and women have fought to bring freedom and justice to those in our world who are oppressed. Thus, allowing these oppressed people to inherit peace in their land and allowing us to continue to live in the peace that we know and experience daily in the United States of America.

Peacemaking is a divine work and we are here to honor those who gave their lives to bring peace to others in our world. We do this as we affirm our conviction and belief that in times like these, our God is present and cares for us. Whatever our ethnic, religious, or political background may be, the fact is our God cares for each of us, especially in times of loss, heartbreak, and tragedy.

I have found the Bible to be a great source of comfort in times like these. For Holy Scripture tells us that God is the source of all comfort, the one who comforts us in our troubles, in our distress, and in our grief. No matter how hard we try, words simply cannot express the horror, the shock, and the pain of such loss. A loss that cannot ever be replaced, but I believe that if our military comrades, spouses, sons, daughters, brothers, sisters, or grandchildren could say one last thing to us, it would be for us to stand tall, to be strong and courageous, to not falter and to have hope. For, I believe they would say to us;

> I have fought the good fight, I have finished the course, I have kept the faith. Henceforth there is laid up for me a crown of righteousness, which the Lord, the righteous judge, shall give me at that day, and not to me only, but unto all... (II Timothy 4:7-8)

This war that we find ourselves engaged in today is a different kind of war, a different kind of battle. Military professionals call it asymmetrical warfare, but it is still a conflict that has the potential to destroy our way of life. We're facing a new kind of enemy. Each of these young men and women knew that in a very real and sober way. And yet, they freely chose as our nation's sons and daughters to stand up against the tyranny that challenges our way of life.

From the very beginning of this nation, Americans have freely called upon God to be present and to bless them, to care for them, and to keep them safe. And so it is with us today, we especially need Him with us in all our endeavors. And we need the help of the Spirit of God. "Yea though I walk through the valley of the shadow of death, I will fear no evil for Thou art with me, Thy rod and Thy staff they comfort me…" and again Holy Scripture reminds us of our hope, our refuge, and a new strength:

> God is our refuge and strength; an ever present help in times of trouble. Therefore we will not fear, though the earth give way, and the mountains fall into the heart of the sea… the God of Jacob is with us… (Psalm 46).

On many different occasions I have heard the question asked, "Where do we get such men and women like these?" Men and women who courageously give sacrificially and unselfishly when the country calls upon them to fight her wars? Men and women who are dedicated to such ideals and who exhibit such commitment? I still believe there is no better answer than the one James Michener gives in his book, *The Bridges at Toko-Ri*, where he says so poignantly,

> Well, we find them where we've always found them. They are the product of the freest society man has ever known. They make a commitment to the military—make it freely, because the birthright we share as Americans is worth defending.

We find them all across this great land, in the rice and sugarcane fields of South Louisiana, on the beaches of Southern California, the inner streets of New York City, the farms, the small businesses and thousands of high schools all across this great land. They are what make this nation so great. These warriors we memorialize today and the thousands of others who serve and have served are the new "greatest generation."

These men and women have indeed been peacemakers like many others before them who took up arms to defend all they believe in and have faith in.

Blessed are the Peacemakers… for they shall be called the children of God.

For it is abundantly clear that these Marines, these sailors, these soldiers whom we honor in this Memorial Service this morning are America's best. They are our husbands and wives, our fathers and mothers, our colleagues, our friends, our buddies, our sons and daughters, our brothers and sisters, our nieces and nephews, and our grandchildren.

They were noble citizens and it must be said that these men and women did do something great in the course of their lives. They committed themselves to their duty and they gave all they had so that peace might have a chance in another part of this world.

I would say that each of them in their own way at different times enjoyed what they did, took pride in their labor, and loved those around them. Through their indomitable spirit, strong character, unwavering example, side splitting humor, and their unquenching love for freedom and all that is holy, right, and just, they brought meaning and purpose to their lives and all who knew them.

They brought peace to a place that knew not peace, to a place that knew not freedom as you and I know it, and hope to a people who had all but given up hope. These Marines, sailors, and soldiers are indeed peacemakers in the greatest sense.

President Dwight D. Eisenhower encapsulates it best in these words:

TO THESE WE OWE THE HIGH RESOLVE THAT THE CAUSE FOR WHICH THEY DIED SHALL LIVE… PEACE, FREEDOM AND JUSTICE!

This morning in closing, I ask you to do one last thing as we honor and remember these brave and honorable Marines, sailors, and soldiers who gave their lives in the service of a grateful nation:

"Think not only upon their passing, but remember the glory of their spirit!"

May the Lord our God bless each of them and may He provide us peace and comfort in the days ahead. God's peace be with you all now and forever. Amen.

Brigadier General James Kessler, USMC, assumed command of 2d Marine Logistics Group, II MEF on 25 May 2006. From January 2007 to February 2008, he deployed the 2d MLG Forward as part of II MEF Forward and MNF-W in support of Operation IRAQI FREEDOM.

Appendix C

Post Traumatic Stress Disorder (PTSD)

Symptoms of PTSD

It is normal to have stress reactions after a traumatic event. Your emotions and behavior can change in ways that are upsetting to you. Even though most people have stress reactions following a trauma, they get better in time. But, you should seek help if symptoms:

- Last longer than three months
- Cause you great distress
- Disrupt your work or home life

What are the symptoms of PTSD?

Symptoms of PTSD may disrupt your life and make it hard to continue with your daily activities. You may find it hard just to get through the day.

There are four types of PTSD symptoms:

1. **Reliving the event (also called re-experiencing symptoms)**
   Memories of the traumatic event can come back at any time. You may feel the same fear and horror you did when the event took place. For example:
   - You may have **nightmares**.

- You may feel like you are going through the event again. This is called a **flashback**.
- You may see, hear, or smell something that causes you to relive the event. This is called a **trigger**. News reports, seeing an accident, or hearing a car backfire are examples of triggers.

2. **Avoiding situations that remind you of the event**
   You may try to avoid situations or people that trigger memories of the traumatic event. You may even avoid talking or thinking about the event. For example:
   - You may avoid crowds, because they feel dangerous.
   - You may avoid driving if you were in a car accident or if your military convoy was bombed.
   - If you were in an earthquake, you may avoid watching movies about earthquakes.
   - You may keep very busy or avoid seeking help because it keeps you from having to think or talk about the event.

3. **Negative changes in beliefs and feelings**
   The way you think about yourself and others changes because of the trauma. This symptom has many aspects, including the following:
   - You may not have positive or loving feelings toward other people and may stay away from relationships.
   - You may forget about parts of the traumatic event or not be able to talk about them.
   - You may think the world is completely dangerous, and no one can be trusted.

4. **Feeling keyed up (also called hyperarousal)**
   You may be jittery, or always alert and on the lookout for danger. You might suddenly become angry or irritable. This is known as hyperarousal. For example:
   - You may have a hard time sleeping.
   - You may have trouble concentrating.
   - You may be startled by a loud noise or surprise.
   - You might want to have your back to a wall in a restaurant or waiting room.

What should I do if I have symptoms of PTSD?
PTSD symptoms usually start soon after the traumatic event. But for some people, they may not happen until months or years after the trauma. Symptoms may come and go over many years. So, you should keep track of your symptoms and talk to someone you trust about them.

If you have symptoms that last longer than four weeks, cause you great distress, or disrupt your work or home life, you probably have PTSD. You should seek professional help from a doctor or counselor.

From: Symptoms of PTSD. (2014, January 3). Retrieved September 1, 2015, from http://www.ptsd.va.gov/public/PTSD-overview/basics/symptoms_of_ptsd.asp

Appendix D

THE NAVY HYMN
Eternal Father, Strong to Save
William Writing
1860

Eternal Father, strong to save,
Whose arm dost bind the restless wave,
Who bidd'st the mighty ocean deep
Its own appointed limits keep;
Oh, hear us when we cry to Thee,
For those in peril on the sea!

O Christ! Whose voice the waters heard
And hushed their raging at Thy word,
Who walked'st on the foaming deep,
And calm amidst its rage didst sleep;
Oh, hear us when we cry to Thee,
For those in peril on the sea!

Most Holy Spirit! Who didst brood
Upon the chaos dark and rude,
And bid its angry tumult cease,
And give, for wild confusion, peace;

Oh, hear us when we cry to Thee,
For those in peril on the sea!

O Trinity of love and power!
Our brethren shield in danger's hour;
From rock and tempest, fire and foe,
Protect them wheresoe'er they go;
Thus evermore shall rise to Thee
Glad hymns of praise from land and sea.

God, Who dost still the restless foam,
Protect the ones we love at home.
Provide that they should always be
By thine own grace both safe and free.
O Father, hear us when we pray
For those we love so far away.

—Hugh Taylor (date unknown)

References

Ballenger-Browning, K. (2010 June). Key facts on resilience. Naval Center for Combat & Operational Stress Control. Retrieved from http://www.med.navy.mil/sites/nmcsd/nccosc/healthProfessionalsV2/reports/Documents/resilienceTWPFormatted2.pdf.

Berger, R. (2015). *Stress, trauma, and posttraumatic growth: Social context, environment, and identities.* New York: Routledge.

Brueggemann, W. (2002). *Spirituality of the Psalms.* Minneapolis, MN: Fortress Press.

Calhoun, G., & Tedeschi, R. G. (2013). *Posttraumatic growth in clinical practice.* New York: Routledge.

Cohen, L. (2009, December 13) *Hallelujah* [Recorded by Bon Jovi]. Retrieved from https://www.youtube.com/watch?v=RSJbYWPEaxw.

Dekel, R., & Solomon, Z. (2007). Secondary traumatization among wives of war veterans with PTSD. In C. R. Figley and W. P. Nash (Eds.), *Combat stress injury: Theory, research, and management* (pp. 137-157). New York, NY: Routledge.

Drescher, K. D., Smith, M. W., & Foy, D. W. (2007). Spirituality and readjustment following war-zone experiences. In C. R. Figley and W. P. Nash (Eds.), *Combat stress injury: Theory, research, and management* (pp. 295-310). New York, NY: Routledge.

Duncan, J. L. (Guest Preacher) (2015, January 25). How Jesus gives us peace. *Sunday Sermon*. Sermon conducted from First Presbyterian Church, Columbia, SC.

Grant, R. (1996). *The way of the wound: A spirituality of trauma and transformation.* Self-published.

Harris, J. I., Park, C. L., Currier, J. M., Usset, T. J., & Voecks, C. D. (2015 January 19). Moral injury and psycho-spiritual development: Considering the developmental context. *Spirituality in Clinical Practice.* http://dx.doi.org/10.1037/scp0000045.

Herman, J. L. (1997). *Trauma and recovery.* New York: Basic Books.

Hogue, C. W. (2010). *Once a warrior always a warrior: Navigating the transition from combat to home—including combat stress, PTSD, and mTBI.* Guilford, CT: Lyons.

Maguen, S. & Litz, B. (2012). Moral injury in veterans of war. *PTSD Research Quarterly, 23* (1). Retrieved from http://sti.mimhtraining.com/wp-content/uploads/2015/02/Fri-1000-Good-Moral-Injury-2012-PTSD-Quarterly-article.pdf.

Marin, P. (1981, November). Living in moral pain. *Psychology today,* 68-80.

Meadors, P. & Lamson, A. (2008) Compassion fatigue and secondary traumatization: Provider self care on intensive care units for children. *Journal of Pediatric Health Care* 22(1): 24-34.

Nouwen, H. J. M. (1972). *The wounded healer: Ministry in a contemporary society.* New York: Doubleday.

Post-traumatic stress disorder (PTSD). (2015). Retrieved from http://www.mayoclinic.org/diseases-conditions/post-traumatic-stress-disorder/basics/definition/con-20022540.

Siemon-Netto, U. (1990). *The acquittal of God: A theology for Vietnam veterans.* Eugene, OR: Wipf & Stock.

Symptoms of PTSD. (2014, January 3). Retrieved from http://www.ptsd.va.gov/public/PTSD-overview/basics/symptoms_of_ptsd.asp.

Tedeschi, R. G., & Calhoun, G. (2004). Posttraumatic growth: Conceptual foundations and empirical evidence. *Psychological Inquiry, 15*(1), 1-18. doi: 10.1207/s15327965pli1501_01.

Thomas, D. W. H. (2014, November 16). A very Scottish Psalm. *Sunday Sermon.* Sermon conducted from First Presbyterian Church, Columbia, SC.

Thomas, D. W. H. (2015, April 5). Does the empty tomb really matter? *Sunday Sermon.* Sermon conducted from First Presbyterian Church, Columbia, SC.

Tick, E. (2005). *War and the soul.* Wheaton, IL: Quest Books.

Walton, H. (2002). Speaking in signs: Narrative and trauma in pastoral theology. *Scottish journal of healthcare chaplaincy* 5(2): 2-5.

Werdel, M. B., & Wicks, R. J. (2012) *Primer on posttraumatic growth: An introduction and guide.* Hoboken, NJ: John Wiley & Sons, Inc.

Whiting, W. (1860) & Taylor, H. (n. d.). Eternal Father, strong to save. Retrieved from http://www.navy.mil/navydata/nav_legacy.asp?id=172.

Biographies

~

CAPT Michael W. Langston, CHC, USN, retired from 36 years of service (30 active) in the U.S. Marine Corps (infantry officer) and the U.S. Navy Chaplain Corps. Receiving a diagnosis of severe PTSD after his tours in Afghanistan and Iraq, CAPT Langston continued on active duty as the Commanding Officer for the Naval Chaplaincy School and Center. His military awards include the Legion of Merit, Bronze Star, and the Defense Meritorious Service Medal. A native of Alabama, CAPT Langston grew up in Lafayette, LA, where he played football for the University of Louisiana in Lafayette. CAPT Langston's educational degrees include: Doctor of Ministry, Master of Arts in National Strategy and Strategic Affairs (Naval War College), Master of Divinity, and Bachelor of Science (Physical Education). Dr. Langston is currently completing his PhD at King's College, University of Aberdeen in Aberdeen, Scotland. He is currently the Professor of Chaplaincy in the Seminary and School of Ministry at Columbia International University.

Kathy J. Langston, PhD, teaches professional communication at the University of South Carolina. A native of Greenville, South Carolina, Dr. Langston embraced military spouse life and enjoyed her ministry with Navy and Marine Corps spouses. Dr. Langston taught university religion and English courses to military students for over fifteen years. Her degrees include: Doctor of Philosophy in English (Composition and Rhetoric), Master of Arts (English—Professional and Technical Writing), Master of Divinity (Languages), and Bachelor of Arts (English). The Langstons are parents of three children: two of whom are in college and one who is a Naval Flight Officer (NFO) in the U.S. Navy and is married with three children. The Langstons have been married over thirty years.

ALSO AVAILABLE FROM
Lampion Press

LOOK FOR THESE AND OTHER
GREAT TITLES AT:

lampionpress.com   LAMPION Press   503.462.3233